Joy and Sorrow

Make My Day – Book 27
Larry M. Henares, Jr.

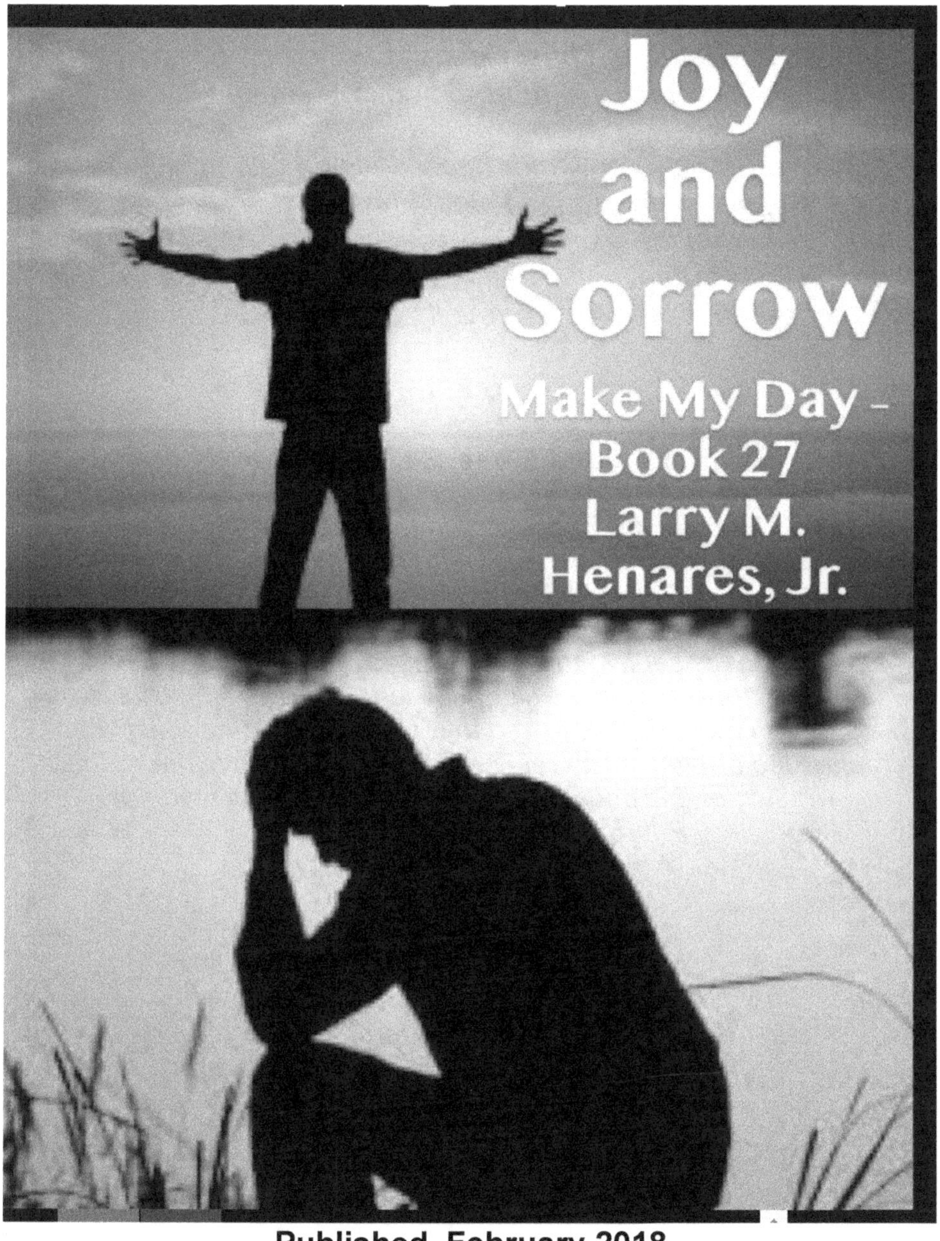

Published, February 2018

Dr. Hilarion M. Henares Jr., known as **Larry Henares,** is a graduate of Ateneo de Manila, University of the Philippines, and the Massachusetts Institute of Technology, an engineer, economist, educator, big businessman, writer, civic leader, public servant, and hobbyist (guns, books, amateur radio and electronics).

He is a writer known for his essays on economics, history, art and culture, a front page columnist in the pre-martial law Manila Times and the most widely read column in the Philippines, according to all surveys, the daily "Make my Day" in the Philippine Daily Inquirer, after the EDSA revolt.

ooooo

Tatay Jobo Elizes, Self-Publisher

This book is published under permission of

DR. HILARION M. HENARES, JR.

Ooooo

About the Book, "JOY AND SORROW"

Here, in this book, the 27th book of the Make My Day Series, Larry Henares waxes poetic about Lea Salonga who won the part of Miss Saigon in London, and Regine Velasquez who refused to play Miss Saigon on Broadway, because her family and neighbors would frown on her making *kandong* and having sex onstage with the leading man.

Here, he also invites the reader to love and lust, to the poetry of the Vagina Monologues and the earthiness of Salitang Puki.

Here, he recounts the attempted assassination of Chavit Singson which was the tipping point that led to the fall of Erap Estrada, and the exciting events leading us to EDSA II when Erap was thrown out from the Presidency though people power. The EDSA II was discussed thoroughly in previous books.

Here, he tells the hilarious story of Juan de la Cruz asking God to make the Philippines a perfect heaven on earth, and his eventual exile to that Pile of Shit that Noah dumped in the far Atlantic.

Here, he tells us why drugs manufactured by American firms are 14 times more expensive in the Philippines, than they are in India. And informs us that while Russia plays the intellectual game of Chess, and China plays the intellectual game of Go, the US plays the visceral game of Poker, bringing bluff and bluster, deceit and instant gratification into international diplomacy.

Here, he exposes the Council of Tent that practically dominates the administration of President Cory Aquino, headed by a Rasputin of a priest, and manned by Cory's Seven Dwarfs, from Doc to Dopey.

Here, he speaks of his daughter's 5 miscarriages, triggered by her immune system that regards the sperm of her husband as a foreign object to be rejected and destroyed – and the advent of Dr. Alan Beer who treated her and brought two pregnancies to term, giving her two sons late in life.

Here, he projects as shadows on the wall, an epic home movie called the Battle of the Sexes in 3 rounds, with a prelude that tells of the creation of Man and Woman, by a mischievous

God; three rounds of (1) a nagging wife, and the secret life of her poor husband, (2) a madcap extramarital affair, and a missing chemise (*camison*); and (3) the Last Supper of a husband and wife, a poisoned glass of wine, and a deadly game of life and death. Add to this a home movie of Somerset Maughm's *Rain* about a priest and a prostitute, and W. W. Jacob's *The Monkey's Paw* and the three wishes that destroyed a family, the characters in both movies played by small children prior to puberty.

Here, in this book, Larry Henares tells the heart-warming story of Teresita Valdez, wife of a policeman, mother of a spoiled only son, supervisor in my wife's factory, who is disliked by all, and whose vocation is to adopt poor children of the streets – eight of them, whom she fed, dressed and sent to school, most of them already abroad in gainful occupations.

Here, he speaks of the Cebuano Enrique, who accompanied Magellan on his trip, from the Moluccas back to Spain, and on his second trip round the Cape of Good Hope to the Philippines. Enrique, claims historian Charlie Quirino, joins Vasco de Gama and Magellan, as the one of the first to circumnavigate the world. He writes of the onerous taxes that eventually kills a nation, of the University of the Philippines, the best school of the country, and why he'd rather send his boys to Ateneo de Manila where he studied. He writes of the balut, the answer to the the great riddle "which comes first the chicken or the egg?" of Greece where Democracy began, of the French Revolution, of the Fall of Spain and the USA which progressed from Barbarism to Decadence without going through the process of being Civilized, and why Hitler hates the Jews.

ooooo

BOOK 27: JOY AND SORROW
TABLE OF CONTENTS

Chapter One: ON STAGE

Part 1. I am a fan of Lea Salonga

Today we honor Bibot Amador of the Repertory Philippines, which gave us our international stars Monique Wilson and Lea Salonga, and five times a week in their William Shaw Theater near Megamall, bathed our world in the light of life and beauty, with echoes of the sad refrain of every great artist:

I burn my candle at both ends,
I will not last the night,
But ah my foes, and oh my friends, --
It gives such lovely light!

The theater is built for the unfolding of dreams. It is the final step in the creative process, where scenes in the imagination and words on a page are given breath and life. It sets the stage for the brief encounter between audience and performer that lasts only for a few hours, and then lives on for a lifetime in memory.
In the theater of my mind there are many beautiful memories of performances that never die, breathless moments of pure magic when the stage spills over to engulf the audience. Specially that of Lea Salonga , except once in They're Playing Our Song..

I once wrote that Lea was perfect as a murderous child in Repertory's "The Bad Seed," and perfect as Miss Saigon, but she is much too cute, much too pretty and too well-bred to be a believable wacky, neurotic, and exasperating Sonia Walsk. Everyone in the audience just wants to hug and kiss her. And Adrian Pang himself is not tall and good-looking enough, and is a little too quirky, with too much facial mugging, to be a straight-laced conservative composer, and without the voice to give the songs a creditable performance. Christopher "Boyet" de Leon was much better as Vernon Gersh. And of course in our imagination, Bernie Villegas is superb as Leon, the offstage neurotic loverboy.

When Cameron Mackintosh, producer of Broadway's greatest hits today -- Cats, Phantom of the Opera, Les Miserables -- went looking for an actress to play the lead role in his new musical Miss Saigon, his search brought him to New York, Los Angeles, Hawaii, his own hometown London, and the Philippines, where a group from Hong Kong and Singapore also auditioned.

He wanted "stunning looks, the voice of an angel, and the operatic stamina of a Pavarotti." In Manila, his search ended. He found not one, but two Miss Saigons -- our very own Lea Salonga and Monique Wilson, plus twelve others for the cast:
They were all good. Jenine is a great singer. Monique is a great actress. Lea is both, and beautiful to boot, with a kind of star quality that made her first choice and won her the Laurence Olivier Award as the best actress in a musical play in all of London.

I am a fan of Lea Salonga. I loved her performance in the play "The Bad Seed" where she played a little girl with a homicidal urge -- long before Macaulay Caulkin in "The Good Son." She was a sensation as Little Orphan Annie in the musical "Annie," better than the Broadway original. And I traveled halfway around the world to see her and Monique Wilson as Kim in "Miss Saigon."

I waxed lyrical when I wrote that she certainly has a star quality and a heavenly voice and that she played Kim as the Caucasians wanted her to, as Madame Butterfly who sacrifices everything for her white lover. On the other hand, I said, though Lea is a better singer, Monique is a better actress, playing Kim as Madam X, a true survivor who sacrifices everything for her child.

To enjoy a play one must be in a relaxed and receptive mood. During Lea's performance, we were still suffering some jet lag, but such was her performance specially in the last act that we were in tears.

Lea is so beautiful it seems no makeup or tears or facial expression can ever give her a look of pain, of suffering, of haggard hopelessness. She has always been our Shirley Temple, as we saw her in "Annie!" It was this quality of innocence that made her such a frightening child murderer in the Bad Seed. She made her mark as a child actress and singer.

Lea interprets Kim beautifully as Innocence caught in the maelstrom of Tragedy, buffeted by forces outside of her control. Monique plays Kim as Courage in face of Misfortune, taking her fate into her own hands, to the very end with her supreme sacrifice.

Lea is Madame Butterfly, Monique is Madame X.

Lea's interpretation is what Westerners want to see. It is their illusion that our Asian women are meek and submissive, sacrificing everything for their honky-white lovers.

Monique's interpretation is what we Asians know our women to be, adventurous, fiercely protective of family, and capable of great sacrifice... like teachers who go as maids to Hong Kong and Saudi, and our nurses in USA and Europe.

No doubt Lea is a star, beautiful, talented, gorgeously desirable. And it's easy to picture her dressed in mink and diamonds, and spirited away by a prince in a Rolls-Royce, pursued by scores of wide-eyed admirers -- leaving her poor mother mired in a hopeless attempt to protect her innocence, her chastity and her childhood. It happened to Shirley Temple and Vilma Santos, it will happen to Lea Salonga.

Magic reigns eternal in the theater of my mind.

October, 2005

Part 2. Lea Salonga wows 'em in *Miss Saigon*

On September 20, 1989, the final version of the play Miss Saigon played to Opening Night audiences at the Theatre Royal Drury with raving reviews, specially about our own Lea Salonga, culminating a month of preview performances, with performances sold out six months ahead.

In Broadway, after the final dress rehearsal of a new play, the whole cast goes "on the road" to many cities around the United States -- Philadelphia, Washington, Boston, Chicago -- actually showing the play to out-of-town audiences before starting its Broadway run in New York.

It is on this Road Show that the play gets its finishing touches, depending on audience reaction, changing scenes, lines, cutting out or adding portions, even changing the actors or actresses.

By the end of Road Show, the play is finely tuned to perfection, the actors seasoned and experienced. Then the Opening Night on Broadway.

In London where Cameron Mackintosh's new play Miss Saigon takes its place among his three other hit shows, Cats, Phantom of the Opera and Les Miserables -- there is no Road Show. There are only a few months of rehearsals and a series of daily "previews" open at a special price to the public, which serves the same purpose as the Road Show, in which the show is interrupted many times, or even stopped.

The play season in London is just beginning. Peter O'Toole is starring in Jeffrey Bernard is Unwell at the Apollo Theatre on October 18th. Tommy Steele is back at the Palladium in Singing in the Rain now until November 11. Leo McKern is Boswell for the Defense at the Playhouse starting September 6. A comedy of sexual errors, Paris Match, started September 20 at the Garrick Theater. And Return to the Forbidden Planet by Bob Carlton, billed as "Shakespeare's Forgotten Rock and Roll Masterpiece," opened September 11.

Baby Barredo, Philippine Queen of the Stage, producer, director, actress of Repertory Philippines, where most of the Filipino actors in the cast of Miss Saigon were trained, was on hand to see many of the preview nights of Miss Saigon, at £18.50 a ticket. So did most Filipinos in Great Britain and the continent, glowing with understandable pride. There were preview shows almost every night, plus a Saturday matinee. There was even a charity night sponsored by the Duchess of Kent, complete with gala gowns and monkey suits, for £1,000 per ticket. And on the eve of the opening, on September 19, the show sponsored by Princess Diana also at £1.000 per ticket.

The play is superbly presented. The setting of the play is Saigon during the Vietnam war, once described by Le Ly Hayslip in When Heaven and Earth Changed Places, thus:

"Saigon was called Paris of the Orient by the French, and like her sister city in Europe, she was sultry and sulky, brash and noisy -- the *yin* and *yang* that produced everything the war became for both sides.

"For the North, she was the symbol of Western decay: a town of whores, corrupt politicians, and greedy citizens who measured themselves more by their resemblance to their foreign masters than by fidelity to their ancestors.

"For the South, she was a shimmering oasis in a desert of fear and poverty. For many Southern peasants to 'go to Saigon' was a passport to unimaginable wealth and excitement."

The play retells the old story of Camille, La Traviata and Madame Butterfly -- of the passionate love of an unworthy woman for a nobleman, and its tragic consequences. Miss Saigon is more like Madame Butterfly.

The play takes place in Saigon in April 1975, in Ho Chi Minh City (formerly Saigon) in April 1978, in Atlanta, Georgia, in

September 1978, in Bangkok in October 1978, with a flashback to Saigon in April 1975.

Act One opens in a Saigon bar owned by a half-caste French-Vietnamese called The Engineer with a chorus singing "The Heat is on in Saigon." Kim orphaned at 15, comes to take a job as a hostess. Here she meets American officer Chris whose friend John arranges with the Engineer ("The Transaction") to have her, still a virgin, sleep with Chris. Kim and Chris fall in love, singing "Sun and Moon," and go through a ceremony of love, singing "Last Night of the World."

The scene shifts to Ho Chi Minh City, three years later, with the coming of communists ("The Morning of the Dragon") and with Kim in her shanty. Magic staging brings down a module from way upstage on to the top of Kim's shanty -- it is an apartment in America where Chris lives with his new American wife Ellen. There ensues a beautiful duet of Kim singing "I Still Believe" that Chris would come back for her, and Ellen believing that Chris is hiding a secret from her, crying out a name from the depths of his dreams.

Thuy, Kim's rejected betroth, comes as a Communist Commissar, and forces The Engineer to bring him to Kim. Kim tells him, "I have a secret" and reveals her love-child Tam with Chris. When Thuy threatened to knife the child, Kim shoots him. And she escapes with the Engineer with the boat people out of Vietnam.

The Second Act begins at the Atlanta Center in Georgia, as John sings a song about the poor Amerasians children left behind in Vietnam, called "Bui-doi" (bidoy). While he is singing this song, on top of the stage appears a film of bui-doi's in a camp in Thailand, "conceived in hell, born in strife, they are the children of the world."

The scene shifts to Bangkok where John meets The Engineer and Kim, and cannot bear to tell Kim that Chris is already married. There is a flashback to the Fall of Saigon in April 1975, "Kim's Nightmare" which shows how Chris and Kim got separated, with Kim waiting while the gates to the helipad closed and Chris forced to leave her behind.

Back at Bangkok, Kim goes to the hotel where Chris was staying, and meets Ellen. Ellen thinks Kim is a maid, Kim thinks Ellen is the wife of John. Learning the truth, Kim leaves, asking that Chris tell her the truth to her own face, and take the child Tam with him to America.

In the final scene, back at her hotel, Kim sings her son to sleep, "The Sacred Bird," and tells him to dream of a better life in America. She puts a baseball cap on him, lays a Mickey Mouse stuffed doll beside him, and leaves the room. Chris comes in with The Engineer, sees his son in bed, and hears a shot in the adjoining room. Kim staggers in and falls into his arms, dying, "Hold me for the last time." They sing a reprise of their love song "Sun and Moon" ending with "how in one night have we gone so far!" The End.

Lea Salonga plays the title role of Kim, with Monique Wilson as her alternate on certain performances. Claire Moore who once played the heroine Christine in Phantom of the Opera, now plays Ellen, the American wife. The romantic lead (Chris) is Simon Bowman who once played the romantic Marius in Les Miserables. Chris' friend John is played by Peter Polycarpou, and Thuy by Keith Burns.

But the biggest role is reserved for the Shakespearean actor Jonathan Pryce who plays The Engineer, a sort of a pimp, bartender and a Greek Chorus -- and who is considered a worthy successor to Laurence Olivier.

In addition to being an alternate to Lea Salonga as Kim, Monique Wilson also plays Mimi, friend of Kim; Isay Alvarez plays Gigi; Pinky Amador plays Yvonne # 1; Jenine Desiderio plays Yvette; Dominique Nobles plays Yvonne # 2; and later Monique, Pinky and Jenine play Go-Go Dancers in the Bangkok scenes.

Junix Inocian plays a Vietnamese soldier; Cocoy Laurel, Miguel Diaz, Jay Ibot, Bobby Martino, William Michaels, and Lyon Roque play Vietnamese customers.

In the Ho Chi Minh City (Saigon renamed by the Communists after the war), Junix Inocian and Miguel Diaz, play Phan and Huynh respectively, North Vietnamese soldiers, as did Bobby Martino, Jay Ibot, Jon Jon Briones, Robert Sena and Lyon Roque; Cocoy Laurel plays the Assistant Commissar.

Later in the Bangkok scenes, Junix, Cocoy, Lyon, and Miguel play The Hustlers.

At the end of the performance, come the curtain calls, from the least to the greatest. First the white actors and two blacks (perfunctory applause); then the Asian actors (applause begin to mount); then the other whites and the romantic lead Simon Bowman; second to the last is our own Lea Salonga (bravo, standing ovation); and the last, Jonathan Pryce (thunderous applause, still standing).

We Filipinos look upon our professional actors as having an American accent. Yet it doesn't sound that way to the whites. They detect a difference in inflection, in modulation, in timbre. They call it the Asian Sound and here in London, they like what they hear. The director, Nicolas Hytner, says that the Filipinos made all the difference in the play.

The Filipino artists live in the artist's colony, Islington, in Greater London. Lea lives with Bebeng Salonga, ever the stage mother, lovingly combing her child's hair and fiercely guarding her chastity. Monique Wilson lives a couple of minutes' walk away, by herself, and looking forward to having her mother Terry Esteva Wilson come from Manila for the opening night.

It is significant that our Filipino actors are making their first big splash in the international stage of the Theatre Royal Drury Lane which epitomizes the British Theatre, now three and quarter centuries on the same site, and the oldest theatre in the world in continuous use as a playhouse since 1663.

Most of the great thespians during the last three hundred years have "trodden the boards of old Drury.' It was built 1663 upon the fall of Puritanism and Cromwell. Burned in 1672, it was rebuilt by the great architect Christopher Wren, and stood for 117 years.

Here acted Baron Booth; James Quinn; David Merrick, acknowledged the greatest English actor in history; Sarah Siddons whose Lady Macbeth established her as one of the greatest tragic actresses of all time. Here the British National Anthem in 1745 and Rule Britannia were first sung. Every English King since Charles II occupied its Royal Box. In 1791 the second Drury Lane was declared unsafe and demolished.

The Third Building (1794-1809) boasted of fire-proof safety curtain, and a vast stage that could contain a large lake with a man rowing a boat. Declared flame-proof, it nevertheless burned down, as Sheridan, its owner, in great distress and outwardly calm, sat drinking, "Leave me, leave me; 'tis a great pity if a man cannot drink a glass of wine by his own fireside."

The Fourth Building was built in 1812 and is still standing after 177 years. It opened with Hamlet preceded by a prologue by Lord Byron. Here George III who lost America, met his son and soundly boxed his ears (on opposite doors may be seen "King's Side' and 'Prince's Side"). Here Edmund Kean started his career as the world's greatest tragedian of all time with an electrifying performance as Sherlock Holmes.

Here the greatest actors and pantomime artists reigned. Here upon the Shakespearean Tercentenary in 1913 George V knighted Frank Benson for his performance in Julius Caesar. Almost all the Broadway plays had their London run here. David Merrick's 42nd Street had 1824 performances, and Pirates of Penzance had 600 performances.

Here the ghost of "The Man in Grey" -- a young man in the costume of the 17th century, powdered wig, tri-cornered hat and wearing a dress sword -- may be seen stalking the Upper Circle seats early in the day. His appearance at the opening night of a new production is considered a good omen.

Here on September 20, 1989, Lea Salonga, Monique Wilson and 12 Filipino thespians were favored by the ghost of "The Man in Grey" and hope to enter the history of international stage as the first and foremost Asian actors of this age.

August 2, 2000, Philippine Post

Part 3.   Lea too cute, too pretty to be wacky, exasperating

They're Playing My Song opened on Broadway on February 1977, a play by Neil Simon, music by Marvin Hamlisch and Carole Bayer Sager, a successful musical about the on-again, off-again relationship between a straight-laced conservative composer, Vernon Gersch, and a wacky neurotic lyricist, Sonia Walsk. The original cast consisted of Robert Klein and Lucie Arnaz, the 4 alter egos of the boy and the 4 alter egos of the girl, performing as a Greek Chorus, and the former boyfriend of the girl named Leon who does not appear on the stage but who reminds us of Bernie Villegas. With a brilliant script and wonderful songs, it was a smash hit.

Lucie Arnaz as the wacky lyricist was perfect for the part of Sonia Walsh. Being the daughter of the greatest TV odd-ball (no pun intended) Lucille Ball, and a Latin drummer, Desi Arnaz, himself a nutty fruitcake, Lucie Arnaz is a wacky neurotic, perfect for the part being played today by Lea Salonga in the Singapore Repertory presentation playing at the AFP Theater, Camp Aguinaldo, from June 20 to August 13, 2000.

Twenty years ago, from May 22 to May 31, 1981, close on the heels of Broadway, a Filipino version was presented at Manila Hotel, with my daughter Juno Henares playing Sonia Walsk and Christopher de Leon, to the plaudits of critics. Sometime later, another version was presented, starring Leah Navarro and Bernardo Bernardo. The present production, imported by Channel 9 blocktimer Felix Co, from Singapore with a Singaporean actor Adrian Pang and manager Gaurav Kripalani, and British director Steven Dexter, tries to duplicate its success in Singapore last year, and succeeds only too well. The response in the Philippines was more polite than enthusiastic, though the audience thoroughly enjoyed themselves watching Lea.

Lea was perfect as a murderous child in Repertory's "*The Bad Seed*," and perfect as Miss Saigon, but she is much too cute, much too pretty and too well-bred to be a believable wacky, neurotic, and exasperating Sonia Walsk. Everyone in the audience just wants to hug and kiss her. And Adrian Pang himself is not tall and good-looking enough, and is a little too quirky, with too much facial mugging, to be a straight-laced conservative composer, and without the voice to give the songs a creditable performance. Christopher "Boyet" de Leon was much better as Vernon Gersh. And of course in our imagination, Bernie Villegas is superb as Leon, the offstage neurotic loverboy.

I won't comment on Juno Henares who is among the more wacky of my children, or Leah Navarro who was my son Ronnie's talent at the time, but I believe the closest thing to Lucie Arnaz in the Philippines is EJ Villacorta, who would expose her breasts on stage for the benefit of my video camera in "*Best Little Whorehouse*," and sing of "Tits and Ass" in "*Chorus Line*," convincingly even though she had none to boast of. EJ is an unmitigated nut who even now plays golf, dressed in bikinis and hair dyed in color purple, who often manages to distract her competitors and win the Cup.

Don't blame Lea for the play, blame Singapore. For decades, Lee Kwan Yu has bred a whole generation of insipid anal people who are afraid to spit on the sidewalk, or scatter cigarette butts, or forget to flush the toilet. In the whole of Singapore there is probably no girl who could play the role of Sonia Walsk. Lea was chosen because she is a great actress and a world celebrity, but her acting is moderated. If she acted well like Lucie Arnaz or EJ Villacorta, she would have been thrown into jail by Lee Kwan Yu.

The Singaporean production of *"They Playing Our Song,"* is bland and insipid, its choreography trite and without creative imagination, its staging too clinically technical and the acting and direction, save that of our own Lea Salonga, without flavor or warmth. But it is still worth seeing.

August 2, 2000

Part 4. Regine: Kissing, grinding, kandong, getting laid

What lengths would you go to be the star of "Miss Saigon"? The irrepressible Martin Nievera was quoted as saying: "I know people who would even kill to get that role. But I personally would do more than that. I would shave my legs, put on a woman's dress and have an operation that will make me sing soprano like a Viennese Choir boy."

It is a good thing Lea Salonga finally got that role on Broadway, because she really deserves it. Winner of the prestigious Sir Laurence Olivier Award for Best Actress in a Musical, for outstanding performances in "Miss Saigon," Lea Salonga was accorded a singular honor as the first Filipino to gain the nod of a British panel of judges.

One recalls painfully that while Filipinas have been consistently winning in practically all beauty contests in the world, from Miss Universe to Miss International, no Filipina ever won in the Miss World contest franchised by the British.

One recalls that when the first prize winner of Miss World was disqualified because she was found to be a mother, the Filipina second prize winner was not allowed to take over the crown and the prizes. One got the impression that the British are not only blind and unfair, but racist as well.

Not only blind, unfair, racist but credit-grabbing also. Considering that the British started this Middle East crisis in 1922, when it carved Kuwait out of Iraq denying the Iraqis access to the sea -- considering that British participation in Operation Desert Storm is not only minor and minimal but quite microscopic -- one wonders why that stuff-shirt British Prime Minister John Major (better named Minor) is upstaging Gorgeous George Bush in issuing television statements and news updates.

Well, talent conquers all. Lea won, and if her alternate Monique Wilson is allowed to qualify, she may also win in the same category in this year. But don't count on it, the British are only good once in a good while.

Lea Salonga, after her West End triumph, was first forbidden by the American Actor's Equity from opening in Broadway. This is only to be expected from Mommie Dearest America whose aging and lack-luster artists are always welcome to perform in Manila and get paid with our precious dollars, courtesy of the IMF, Jess Estanislao and Joey Cuisia.

But talent conquers all, as we said before. And Lea Salonga is now welcomed to Broadway and the Great White Way. We wish her all the luck, and expect her to render us more honors by winning the Tony Award.

But before Lea became the official Broadway star, producer Cameron MacIntosh went on another sortie to interview and audition thousands of aspirants for the role of Kim, both in the United States and Manila. And thereby lies a tale.

What would you do if you were a local girl offered a chance to be the star of "Miss Saigon"? Suppose you initially do not want to audition because you are busy with your concert, and because you made up your mind you are not interested in Miss Saigon for some reason or other?

Suppose Cameron MacIntosh's agent here, Dong Alegre, says: "Look, what is wrong with showing off what you can do to Vinnie Lief, casting director of Miss Saigon? without any obligation on your part to accept any role, or any promise on our part to offer you a role?"

And your manager says, "Well, what the hell, just show them what you can do in a private audience in Manila Hotel suite, not in a public with the others at the CCP, so that it will be understood that this is no audition. And talk to these people, so you will have a good idea of what you are turning down."

So you go to Manila Hotel for a private audience, and sing a couple of songs from Miss Saigon with your expressive, clear and powerful voice trained with sea pressure against your diaphragm, and capable of raising the rafters in the biggest

Broadway theater. And Vinnie Lief, who was also the casting director of "Dream Girls" and "Phantom of the Opera" is impressed, and promised to give his "100 percent recommendation to Cameron MacIntosh!"

Then a few weeks later, surprise of surprises, came an invitation to New York to show off your talent to MacIntosh himself. But you say you are still not interested in Miss Saigon.

Your manager says to you: "For goodness sakes, here is your chance to go to New York for the first time, expense-free, and see America!"

And to Dong Alegre, he says: "I am going to convince her to go to New York, but I want to tell you as her manager that in case she is interested, the only thing that will make it worthwhile is a crack at the major role as Kim in Broadway."

And Dong answers: "Well, there is no offer yet, but obviously Vinnie Lief thinks she is a natural even without stage experience, and MacIntosh wants to see her, so what can you lose?"

In three meetings, against the wishes of your mother, your manager convinces you that while you may not like Miss Saigon, you may be offered something else you like. And you go to New York with the clear understanding with Dong Alegre that you will keep your options open.

So you go to Broadway, and see all the musical plays, and say, "I love the Phantom of the Opera! If I am offered the role of Christine, I'll scream with joy!"

You sing for MacIntosh, and by golly you get another invitation from MacIntosh to go to London for voice coaching, with the hope that your concert style may be adjusted to the musical stage.

If you pass this test, then you are half a step away from a major Broadway role. This time Dong Alegre said, "Well, we have gone this far, so you must be prepared to accept if offered the role."

Suppose you were this lucky person, what would you say? I am sure that if you were columnist Richard F. Lo or Nestor Cuartero, you will repeat what Martin Nievera said, shave your legs, put on a woman's dress and submit to orchiectomy.

But you are not Lo or Cuartero, you are in truth the singing sensation Regine Velasquez, and you tell Dong Alegre, "No thank you, I am not going!" And nobody believes you, you must be kidding, people would give their front teeth for a role in Miss Saigon.

And you, Regine, would say No? You must be sour-graping because no definite offer has been given to you. You must be afraid that in the end, you will prove not good enough and be rejected. So Lo and Cuartero wrote in their columns, and you are hurt and devastated, you wish you did not go to Manila Hotel and Broadway.

And you explain: "After being invited to New York, I was subsequently invited by MacIntosh to London, so I must have had a pretty good chance to get the role.

"Sure I might be rejected in the end, but I have never been afraid to lose. I lost more singing contests than the 67 contests I won with first prize.

"I did not go because I just don't feel right (*hindi bo-o ang loob ko*) about the role of Kim, with all the kissing, grinding, panties showing, *kandong* (twining my legs around the guy's waist), getting laid in bed and pretending to do the sex act. *Nandidiri ako.*

"I am a *provinciana* who still lives in a Bulacan barrio, and my neighbors as well as my own mother, think the role is obscene and destructive of my morals. I cannot help it, their opinion of me is the most important thing in the world at this time of my life. I may become more sophisticated later, but today I am a prude.

"Here in the Philippines I can foresee the path of my career clearly far into the future, but I cannot foresee what happens to me in Broadway after Miss Saigon. I am afraid to be alone, by myself, away from my family in a strange country, where the life-style is unfamiliar and threatening.

"And at present I am earning more money from my concerts than I could possibly earn in Broadway.

"Lea is a city girl, she can adjust, and she is better as a stage actress than I am."

If it is any consolation to you, Regine Velasquez, you are better as a concert artist. Lea Salonga is an accomplished singer, polished and professional on the legitimate stage, but in concerts she never was able to make me cry in exultation, as you do when echoes of your "*Narito Ako*," "*Ebbtide*" and "*Somewhere Out There*" like Handel's Hallelujah, stagger the mind into thoughts of Time, Space, Eternity and God.   *February 8, 1991*

Chapter Two: THE MATING GAME

Part 1. An invitation to love, lust, sex and procreation

Faces are exquisite instruments of expression. Behind our facial skin lies an intricate web of muscles, 22 of them on each side of the face, especially around the eyes and the mouth, that can be called upon to produce 10,000 different expressions - - love, hate, fear, joy, ecstasy, contentment, surprise, doubt, distrust, suspicion, interest and countless other emotions.

Evolved purely for a social communication, each emotion can be further modified by the raise of an eyebrow or the slight flick of a cheek muscle to express, say, measured surprise, wild surprise, disappointed surprise, feigned surprise, etcetera.

Among these signals are formal invitations to potential mates, called flirtations. *"'Tis not a lip, or eye, we beauty call,/ but the joint force and full result of all,"* wrote Alexander Pope. On the anatomy of the face of a woman we can see the "joint force" that perpetuates the human race -- the shy smile, the bashful lowering of a gaze to one side and down, followed by a furtive look at the man's face, the unobtrusive wetting of the lips - - the same on the face of a Tasaday tribeswoman and a sophisticated Makati secretary

The human mate-recognition system is overwhelmingly visual. "Love comes in at the eye," wrote Yeats, and the locus of the human body that lures the eye most of all is the face -- a trait our species shares with many other primates. "It is a common Old World anthropoid ploy," says Masters. "Cercopithecoid monkeys have brightly painted faces with species-specific patterns, which they wave like flags in the forest gloom. Good old evolution tinkering away, providing new variations on a theme." Humans love to mate. The barriers between races melt away when sex is at stake. This according to James Shreeve in his article "The Neanderthal Peace" (Discover, September, 1995), which we excerpt above.

The face make-up, the sexy dress, the slight touch of the hand and whole gamut of body language are there to embellish one grand design -- an invitation to love, lust, sex and procreation -- no matter how modified by layers and layers of civilized behavior, born of culture, religion, and social convention.

A universal signal sent to all is intended to be received only by a selected few. Let those beware who respond and are not appreciated, because they are likely to be accused of sexual harassment, hounded by modern society, shamed by the thought that they were called but not welcomed.

There are few ideal couples like movie stars and the jet set, destined for happiness by heaven itself, then condemned to the hell of separations, divorce and multiple marriages. The irony is that the desirable women only want desirable men and vice-versa. The educated ones, the beautiful and the handsome, the best and the brightest, the rich and the powerful, gravitate toward each other.

And the rest of humanity are left to choose from the second-best, the dregs, the leavings, the residuals, the residues. The human race is fast devolving separately into the beautiful and the ugly, the brightest and the moronic, the rich and the poor, the good and the bad, the loved and the unlovable.

Part 2. The call of the wild and wet and wonderful

The perpetuation of the race of any species begins with a mating call: the call of the wild and wet and wonderful. This message will only be heard within the same species and no other. So writes James Shreeve, in an article published in the September 1995 issue of *Discover*, "The Neanderthal Peace," which we excerpt.

"It may be a chemical, sent out by the eggs of the brown alga Ascophyllum nodosum, for example, which attracts the sperm of A. nodosum and no other. It may be the color, perfume and nectar of a flower attracting insects to bring the pollen from the stamen to the pistil. Or a vaginal smell like that of a bitch in heat which attracts all the male dogs in the vicinity, but not tomcats or teen-age boys. Girls and boys of the human race recognize visual signals that call for the wild and wet and wonderful, leading to the perpetuation of the species, but only of human beings.

"A female of one species might hear the song of the male of another species," explains Judith Masters of the University of Witwatersrand , "but she won't make any response. There's no need to talk about what *prevents* her from mating with that male. She just doesn't see what all the fuss is about."

Adaptations to the local habitat may influence the evolution of the species, but not as much as any change in the mate-recognition system. A sparrow born with a slightly too short beak may or may not be able to feed its young as well as another with an average size beak, but if he can attract a mate, his kind may yet survive. But a sparrow who sings an unfamiliar song will not attract a mate and is not going to have any young at all. He will be plucked from the gene pool of the next generation, leaving no evolutionary trace of his idiosyncratic serenade. The same goes, of course, for any sparrow hen who fail to respond to potential mates singing the "correct" tune.

"The only time a species' mate recognition system will change is when something really dramatic happens," Master says. For such a drama to unfold, a population must be geographically isolated from its parents. If the population is small enough and the habitat radically different from what it was previously, even the powerful evolutionary inertia of the mate-recognition system may be overcome. This change in reproduction maybe accompanied by new adaptations to the environment. Or it may not. Either way the only shift that marks the birth of the new species is the one affecting the recognition of mates. Once the recognition threshold is crossed, there is no going back. Even if individuals from the new population and the old come to live in the same region again -- let's say in a well-trafficked corridor of fertile land linking their two continental ranges -- they will not longer view each other as potential mates."

And James Shreeve theorizes, that is the reason why the Neanderthal Man and the Cro-Magnon Man, two radically different types of humans, thought to be following each other in the sequence of evolution, were surprisingly found to be existing side by side in Spain for perhaps 50,000 years. And for all those thousands of years, the two apparently had nothing to do with each other, no sexual intercourse, no common call for the wild, wet and wonderful.

January 17-18, 1996, ISYU

Part 3. Are workplace romances good for business?
Some offices forbid as a matter of policy any workplace romance that interfere with its main business. Well, not exactly, because in the last analysis, the mating game and the pursuit of

happiness are a human right protected by international treaties and a constitutional right protected by the basic law of the land. But some companies insist that the man and wife in their payroll must work in different departments, or one of them should resign. Some companies tolerate romances between equals but not between superior and underling, as practiced in the Armed Forces, because it is not compatible with line discipline, and it is liable to deteriorate into a sexual harassment suit. By law, such offense only occurs between a superior who has control, and the underling.

My son Atom who has many company offices to run, believes in the axiom that office work should not be brought into the home, and conversely, work in the home should not be brought to the office. Every person in the office should be required to wear a chastity belt during work, and hang it up with his work card when he punches out at the end of the working day. Atom notices an internal breach of discipline among office workers in love and the people around them:

1. When the couples have a lover's quarrel and infect others.

2. When there are jealousies among rivals in the courtship.

3. When the female has her menstruation, and becomes moody.

4. When fellow workers accuse loving couples of favoring each other.

5. Whether fulfilled or frustrated, reciprocal or unrequited, it infects the entire atmosphere of stable office relationships.

6. When hidden relationships and gossiping interfere with work.

Generally, a couple who spend the whole night together at home suffer the boredom of seeing each other throughout the working day. Too much is simply too much, proving the validity of the saying that absence makes the heart grow fonder. I kid you not, most of the romance evaporates after overexposure.

The mating game redefined by the rules of sexual harassment is simply unfair to the male of the species. The female insists on her traditional role as the reluctant virgin, playing hard to get, and *hele-hele bago quiere*, while the male has absolutely no idea if his attentions are welcomed or not. If after being kissed or what-not, she decides she did not like it, the boy having halitosis or body odor, she may now institute proceedings against sexual harassment. If on the other hand, she really enjoyed the kiss and what-not, she may respond with a flick of the tongue, a press of the fingers or body motion, but she rarely abandons her "hard to get" role. There are reasons for this (1) her reluctance goads the boy further into the trap (first a woman resists a man's advance, then in the end, she blocks his retreat); (2) she sidesteps the entire blame for committing a mortal sin (I'm sorry, Father, I resisted but he forced me!), (3) Most girls look upon sexual advances as a test of how attractive they can be (Look, I may not like it coming from him, but I hope he tries anyway, it's good for my ego).

Generally, according to my son Atom, putting males and females together in the office is potentially explosive. The proximity of the couples and the duration of their exposure to each other simply are a challenge to do what comes naturally. And when the relationship reaches critical mass, watch out for the inevitable chain reaction. Atom's right, wear a chastity belt to work.

September 20, 1999, Philippine Post

4. The Vagina Monologues, fact sheet

According to the author Eve Ensler, "I was worried about vaginas. I was worried about what we think about vaginas, and even more worried what we don't think about them... So I decided to talk to women about their vaginas, to do vagina interviews, which became vagina monologues. I talked with hundreds of women. I talked to old women, young women, married women, single women, lesbians, college professors, actors, corporate professionals, sex workers, African American women, Hispanic women, Asian women, Native American women, Caucasian women, Jewish women. At first, women were reluctant to talk. But once they got going, you couldn't stop them."

The Vagina Monologues is precisely what its name suggests -- a series of stories, based on interviews, in which women talk about the most secret part of their bodies. But it's a great deal more. The author, Eve Ensler shows so triumphantly that by opening up such a subject, you can also reveal a whole range of human experience. Using intelligence, integrity and compassion, Ensler has created not just one of the best shows in the world today (it has premiered in over 15 countries and translated in over 10 languages) but the most morally serious. In The Vagina Monologues, Eve Ensler has given voice to a chorus of lusty, outrageous, poignant, brave, highly original and thoroughly human stories. Based on interviews with a diverse group of women -- the play brazenly explores the humor, power, pain, wisdom, outrage, mystery and excitement hidden in vaginas. Having seen The Vagina Monologues, no one -- woman or man -- will ever look at the world the same way again.

The Vagina Monologues has been called "a bona fide phenomenon" (The New York Times), "alternately funny, poetic and provocative" (Entertainment Weekly), "marvelous, one of the best shows in town" (Daily News) and "a work of art and a piece of cultural history" (Variety). Eve Ensler has become a phenomenon because of her monologues about a body part. A body part that 30 years after the sexual revolution people are still embarrassed about naming aloud.

The Vagina Monologues is alternately hilarious and deeply moving. But as important as the serious monologues are -- like the piece about Bosnian rape victims and childbirth -- humor is the shows' real strength. Covering issues from sexual abuse, first lesbian experiences, indignities or pelvic exams, women's dreams, orgasms and sex among others, the play deftly combines drama and comedy. The play's language is frank and open, and the stories it tells are vivid and direct. Both remain rooted in real characters and recognizable experiences.

5. If the vagina can talk, what will it say?

No, not Virginia. It is Vagina, The Vagina Monologues, the hottest play on Broadway, that is coming to town. It is Eve Ensler's controversial play, where one woman with two others takes center stage with a series of monologues based on interviews with real women on the subject of their most intimate body part, the vagina. But it's a great deal more. For the author shows that by opening up such a subject, you can also reveal a whole range of human experience. Seeing the play itself is a moving experience. Women will liberate themselves from all the taboos that hold them captive all their lives. Men probably for the first time will know and appreciate what it is to be a woman, to appreciate everything that goes on inside her, from menstruation to penis penetration to rape, to the conception, growth in the womb and the birth of a baby, and menopause.

If the vagina could talk what would it say? In Broadway, the author Eve Ensler herself -- in Metro Manila in the Music Museum on September 7, 8, and 9, our very own Monique Wilson -- would sit on a stool sheathed in black, with a few lighting effects, and soar to Rabelaisian heights with a bravura impression of every type of orgiastic moan, or move us with quiet compassion with the story of a woman in her 70s describing the embarrassing episode in a car as a teenager that all but ended her relationship with the place "down there". There's a woman who thinks she lost her clitoris while swimming; there's the very funny story about "a woman who had a good experience with a man."

With passion and control, Ensler takes us into the mind of an abused child, a sexually abused homeless woman, and of a victim of mass rape in Bosnia, waxing lyrical about her ravaged vagina. She draws on conversations with women who are young and old, black and white, American and foreign, gay and straight, rich and poor -- real characters with recognizable experiences unfolding a dazzling range of emotions — from gutsy exuberance to fierce anger to poignant reflection. If their stories are offensive, then so is life itself. Next comes a vignette about a happy and fulfilled "sex worker with women only." A final rhapsody on a witnessed birth at last achieves a climax of poetry and power.

The political activism of Eve Ensler blossomed out of a troubled youth. She has described being abused physically and sexually by her father while growing up in Scarsdale, N.Y. She turned to alcohol in high school and, after Middlebury College in Vermont, wandered the country in a haze before cleaning herself up and starting to write. Her social-activist pieces keep coming: *Borrowed Light*, an evening of the writings of women prisoners that she conceived and directed; a one-woman show about nuclear disarmament and another based on the stories of homeless women. Her play *Necessary Targets*, was drawn from the accounts of Bosnian rape victims, with whom she spent 10 days one summer gathering stories about women's experiences during the war ("I came back and just cried for a week"). Next year she is planning to tour in a new piece, *Points of Re-Entry*, about the ways women mutilate their bodies to satisfy cultural norms, from Thai women who wear heavy metal braces to elongate their necks to American teens who starve themselves to stay thin. Married once and divorced, she legally adopted her former stepson, actor Dylan McDermott.

Vagina Monologues is played with a rotating roster of stars that includes Glenn Close, Winona Ryder, Rita Moreno, Rosie Perez, Marisa Tomei, Susan Sarandon, Whoopi Goldberg, Lily Tomlin, Kate Winslet, Melanie Griffith, Marsha Mason, and Brooke Shields. On September 7-9 in the Music Museum, will play Monique Wilson, Tami Monsod and Dulce Aristorenas; later a different roster of actresses (my daughter Juno Henares-Chuidian would love to be in it) leading up to V-DAY 2001 at Madison Square Garden in New York where the Philippine production will be a participant.

September 4, 2000, Philippine Post

6. Vagina Monologues, *Salitang Puki*

You should see it, the world-famous Vagina Monologues, in Filipino, at the Music Museum, in Greenhills, San Juan, starring Pinky Marquez, Arlene Borja and Harlene Bautista-Sarmienta. It is much better than the English version. A series of monologues performed off-Broadway by famous stage and screen stars such as Brooks Shields, Whoopi Goldberg and Candice Bergen, the Monologue was performed in English here in Manila, even better by Monique Wilson and Tamy Monsod, simply because Filipinos are warmer, more malibog, and more expressive than Anglo-Saxons who always seem more dispassionate, detached and repressed in comparison.

In Filipino the Monologues sound even better, more earthy, more moving, more resonant with words that sound like their meaning – onomatopoeia, we call it. *Halinghing*, a Filipino word meaning orgasm, which sounds like the moans of the sexual climax, is used with hilarious effect by Arlene Borja featuring the various sounds of female orgasm. The audience is teased with questions like: If your vagina got dressed what would it wear? If your vagina could talk, what would it say? What does your vagina smell like? All these much more intimate and personal with the substitution of *puki* for vagina which is a medical term.

Tinggil, meaning clitoris, mutilated in the wilds of Africa was described with horrid effect by Harlene. How pathetic was the account of Arlene Borja about the husband who wanted his wife's pubic hair cleanly shaven, so he can enjoy a pedophile's desire, how she was repelled by the hairy pubic hair grinding her soft skin raw like a sandpaper. Yet she acquiesced on the advice of a marriage counselor who warned her that her refusal might tempt her husband to go *"kaliwa."* She consented, his razor nicked her soft spot, she endured the blood and the pain, and then later revealed that her husband *"nangaliwa pa rin siya."*

Almost in awe. Pinky Marquez tells of on ordinary unexceptional fellow, with an exceptional habit, of staring at her vagina in the full light of day, *"dahil gusto niya nitong tingnan,"* enjoying the sight for hours while she fidgets and says: *"Tama na yan. Gawin mo na ang dapat mong gawin."*

There was the heart-breaking story by Harlene of a little girl with *"mimosa pudica,"* in Latin, the flower of modesty, meaning the virginal hymen, which her mother advised her to keep pure and unstained. At six, a bedpost hit it while she was jumping on her bed, at ten she was raped by her father's best friend who was shot by the father while he was on top of her. She shut her *puki* out of her mind until she gained fulfillment in the arms of an older woman who was friendly, beautiful and a lesbian.

The most accomplished actress of the three was Harlene Bautista, sister of the vice-mayor of Quezon City, who performed two of the demanding roles of the Monologues: the woman raped by Bosnian soldiers as a political statement, and a grandmother watching the birth of her grandchild. The rape by Bosnian soldiers, reminiscent of the abuses in Mindanao, probably kept in the original to avoid offending the abusive soldiers of our own army, was described by Harlene with all its horrors, "like being skewered with dead animal corpses inside her body." And the birth of a child coming out of the portal of a woman's body is described by Harlene, *"Naroon ako sa silid,"* in awed tones of sheer power and poetry.

See the *Salitang Puki* in the Music Museum in Greenhills this Friday and Saturday. Your last chance. After this it will go on tour in the USA.

October 13, 2010

ooooo

Chapter Three: THE MILITARY

Part 1. The militarization of our democracy

To be sure there are soldiers who rose above their calling and in many ways become outstanding statesmen. Pericles of Athens who nurtured democracy in ancient Greece, Julius Caesar who brought Pax Romana and law and order to the barbarians, Napoleon Bonaparte who gave the Napoleonic Code and the metric system to Europe, Colonel Abdul Nasser who revived Arab pride and challenged western imperialism, General Charles de Gaulle who liquidated the French colonies and strengthened a democracy threatened by a rebellious military, General Dwight D. Eisenhower who ended the McCarthyist anti-Communist hysteria in the USA – and the gentle General Emilio Aguinaldo who declared our Independence, made us a nation and fought two colonial powers, and our very own General Fidel V. Ramos who restored the people's faith in democracy and made us emerge as a new Asian Economic Tiger.

But these are exceptions to the rule. Soldiers are by their nature the antithesis of the democratic man. Militarizing our democracy or as General Arturo Enrile puts it, democratizing the military are oxymoronic contradictions in terms.

Most of the problems of today's democracies are their military. In Indonesia, Thailand, Korea, Angola, Nigeria, Guatemala, Argentina, Haiti, and many unfortunate countries, they violate human rights with impunity, and persecute without due process political dissidents in behalf of the CIA and half-assed dictators.

In the Philippines, what was a small disciplined and patriotic force of 60,000 soldiers before the Martial Law, became an unwieldy 260,000 that used up a third of government expenditures, took over civilian jobs, and harbored criminal elements that robbed banks, carnapped cars, provided murder for hire, killed and mutilated the enemies of Marcos and the United States.

After Martial Law, the military that helped depose the dictator, remained intact and very vocal about what it wants for the country. It became politicized, sabotaging the peace talks with dissidents, staging several attempts at a coup d'etat, some plotting to bring back the dictator, others terrorizing voters into electing anti-communist goons into office, endorsing the Low Intensity Conflict (LIC) bloodbath doctrines of the lunatic fringe, supporting the retention of American bases in the Philippines, and above all, betraying a persistent desire to institute ``emergency measures" to deal with the insurgency.

Due to the loyalty of Defense Secretary Fidel Ramos and the even-handed rule of President Corazon Aquino, our democracy has prevailed. But three lessons were derived from our experience with our military.

First is the realization that the soldier is by the necessity of his calling the antithesis of a democratic citizen. For a soldier must submit to the disciplines of a rigid military organization that is essentially dictatorial and non-democratic. All their lives, soldiers took orders and gave orders, without doing any thinking in between, which we citizens are called upon to do. *Theirs' not to reason why, theirs' but to do or die*, according to poet Lord Alfred Tennyson, in his *Charge of the Light Brigade*. Soldiers are necessary to protect us democratic citizens from our enemies. But who will protect us from our protectors when they abuse us?

Second is what President Aquino said to her soldiers: "Your only job is to fight our enemies. Your only obligation is to fight well. Leave politics to the civilians." What she meant to say was this: "As a soldier you must submit to the civilian supremacy. Do not argue with us with a gun in your hand. If you want to argue, lay down your arms and be a civilian. Then argue with us in open free and unlimited debate."

Third is that the military is being paid and armed by the people for one reason only: to uphold the majesty of the law and human rights of the citizens. When dissidents violate human rights, they commit a culpable crime and must be caught and punished by the police and the military. When the military violates human rights, there is no force extant that can punish them. When the military violates human rights, it is not only a crime, it is a travesty of the majesty of the law, worse it is a betrayal of the people's trust, it is treason. Such is the stuff of which *coup d'etats* are made of, it deserves no amnesty, it cries out for justice, not mercy. And certainly, notwithstanding what General Jose Almonte declares, except for a few, military men are far less qualified than civilians in running a democratic government.

Part 2. General Charles de Gaulle is so unlike General Joe Almonte

On May 5, 1954, following a disastrous war to contain communism by bloodbath as was also practiced by the USA, France was defeated by the Vietminh forces at Dien Bien Phu.

Then as among the RAMboys and most military men, the French Army blamed the politicians of France for their defeat. Clinging to their dreams of empire, they fought the rebels of Algeria, and at the brink of defeat, again blaming the French government, they threatened a coup d'etat from Algeria.

On June 1, 1958, the French Assembly invited General Charles De Gaulle, World War II hero, to return as premier with extraordinary powers.

De Gaulle refused, he asked instead for the ratification of a new constitution and his direct election as the President of France.

As president he negotiated peace with a free Algeria, aligned himself with the Third World neutral nations, exploded the first French atom bomb, recognized China (the first western nation to do so), took France out of the American dominated NATO, and expelled all American troops out of his country.

The Americans hated him as much as they did the Russians, but they had to respect him, as they never respected Bernardo Villegas and the religious freaks, senators and soldiers who favored the American bases and served them with canine loyalty.

President de Gaulle made a clear distinction between his role as President of France and as leader of the Free French Armies during the war.

He insisted on civilian supremacy, and would not take office unless elected directly by the people. And when his long-cherished plan of electoral reform was defeated by referendum, he interpreted that as lack of confidence and resigned irrevocably.

His concept of a soldier is that he is the security guard of the republic under the direct command of the President, not a man of destiny who rattles the sword every time he disagrees with government policy. He put rebellious French generals in their place and threatened to have them shot if they so much as point a gun at a civilian.

Unlike General Joe Almonte, de Gaulle did not believe that the military has any special qualities of mind and character that make them superior to the civilian. Unlike General Joe Almonte he did not believe that the military has any special role to play as partners of politicians to steer the country towards a "socialist revolution," socialism only meaning the transfer of power and wealth from the lords of land and industry to the more undeserving generals He knew from the experience of others that military domination of national life only means more corruption, more unpunished crime and violation of human rights.

And he never appointed a military man in an important civilian government position. De Gaulle is right and Almonte is wrong, as evidenced by the very examples cited by Almonte for emulation: South Korea, Taiwan, Thailand, and Indonesia, where militarism resulted in political oppression and corruption. As evidenced by our own experience during the period of Martial Law.

Part 3.   The soldier is almost an anomaly in a democracy

General de Gaulle's concept of a democracy is an open-ended society where leftists and rightists are welcomed to sell their ideas in open free and unlimited debate. He would have never appointed a militarist to the cabinet, there to fulminate on the presence of leftists in government, and to unleash the vigilantes to behead anyone disagreeing with those who squat on the status quo. President de Gaulle had this to say about the role of the soldier:

Men who adopt the profession of arms submit of their own free will to a law of perpetual constraint, of their own accord. They reject their right to live where they chose, to say what they think, to dress as they like.

From the moment they become soldiers, it needs but one order to settle them in this place, to move them to that, to separate them from their families, and dislocate their normal lives.

In the world of command, they must rise, march, run, endure bad weather, go without sleep or food, be isolated in some distant post, work till they drop.

They have ceased to be the master of their fate. If they drop in their tracks, if their ashes are scattered to the four winds, that is all part and parcel of their job.

In many ways, a good soldier is one of the most admirable men in the world, like a good priest almost. Like the priest he is bound to strict discipline and self-sacrifice; he risks a lot for little monetary gain.

But he is almost an anomaly in a democratic society. He is the very antithesis of the democratic man. He must never question why, or reason why; if he does, he weakens the efficiency and effectivity of army discipline. His is but to do or die.

As such he is necessary to the survival of our democratic society. We need him to protect us from our enemies. But who is to protect us from our protectors, if they betray our trust and violate our human rights?

It is important that our democratic society demand the complete loyalty of the soldier. The soldier's loyalty to our President and commander-in-chief must be complete and unassailable. Otherwise, our society is in danger.

Elbert Hubbard once gave this advice on loyalty to his colleagues, an advice government employees, especially soldiers should seriously ponder.

If you work for a man, in heaven's name, work for him. Speak well of him and stand by the institution which he represents.

Remember, an ounce of loyalty is worth a pound of cleverness. If you must growl, condemn and eternally find fault, resign your position.

And when you are outside, damn to your heart's content. But as long as you are part of the institution, do not condemn it. For if you do, the first high wind that comes along will blow you away. And you probably will never know why.

Colonel Gringo Honasan and his misguided soldiers should know by now why, in the high winds of fury that followed the morning of Aug. 28, they were simply blown away.

Part 4. So why does Ramos appoint the military to civilian positions?

General Renato de Villa, General Arturo Enrile, General Jose Magno, and all the others of military caste, even General Jose Almonte himself, may assume that they were appointed to their present positions by President Fidel Ramos, because they are retired from the military, and that military men have special qualities of mind and character that make them better than civilians – but they would be wrong.

They would be wrong because President Ramos does not think the way they do. Ramos is no army brat, his entire family background is far from being military – his father was a newspaperman and public servant, his mother a teacher and civic leader, his sister a diplomat and a senator, and no one in his immediate family including his children, is a soldier. He is the one and only soldier in a civilian family of prominence. He couldn't possibly think soldiers are the best and the brightest. Hahaha, that is the most ridiculous notion ever to emerge from the mind of General Almonte – who is obviously his own example.

They would be wrong because they were appointed by Ramos in spite of and not because they are military men. They were appointed because they were formerly the colleagues and friends of Ramos throughout his productive life – because they are the people with whom he worked in the past, whose talents he appreciates, and whose honesty and competence he has confidence in. Being from the military is irrelevant, If Ramos were a big businessman elected to the presidency, he would have chosen colleagues and competitors in the world of business.

Every head man, whether corporate or military or plain civilian, chooses his team from among those he respects and appreciates. Of all presidents, according to oppositionist Arturo Tolentino, Diosdado Macapagal had the best cabinet members, because he admired, respected and trusted all he appointed and avoided having his family involved in government. President Marcos had a good cabinet, but he corrupted and bullied them into being inutile.

On the other hand, President Cory Aquino, having been a housewife, had no pool of talents to choose from, and had to rely on the recommendations of her politician relatives (particularly her brother), her daughter and her friends, her son-in-law, her business adviser and his business colleagues, and worst of all, her father confessor. She had the worst cabinet that ever was, uncontrollable and pulling in different directions, subservient to the Americans, and totally incapable of rendering the most basic services, like electricity, water and telephones, and peace and order.

President Ramos I know would have preferred to have in his cabinet competent and honest civilians, but he does not have any experience with most of them, and those he appointed upon the recommendation of his political colleagues and business supporters, proved to be disappointing to the public -- like Hilarion Ramiro, Boy Blue del Rosario, Sonny Garcia, Amado Lagdameo, and Peter Garrucho. But the people with whom he worked all his life, mostly military men and Pangalatoks, somehow survived the ordeal.

One of the best sources from whom to choose one's team, is one's own classmates, of whom one knows from years of experience those who are bright, competent, honest, dependable and cooperative, as well as who are absolute morons, squealers, bloodsuckers and cheaters. Joe Almonte's *Mein Kampf* opinion notwithstanding, I am sure there are many many military men President Fidel Ramos would happily appoint to a government office when and only when bananas start to grow in the North Pole.

April 25-30, 1997, ISYU

ooooo

Chapter Four:
THE FALL OF ERAP ESTRADA

Part 1. Was Chavit Singson a target for assassination?

On the night of October 3, 2000 at about 11:00 PM, along San Marcelino towards United Nations Avenue, the car of Ilocos Sur Governor Luis "Chavit Singson was blocked by two police patrol cars and a red private vehicle. Twelve heavily armed men with Armalites, demanded that he open the door and step out of the car. The governor instinctively knew his life was in danger. He knew that if he left the car, he may be met by a hail of bullets from armed men who will later claim he pulled a gun on them. He himself was a victim of 11 ambuscades in the past. In one he lost 9 of his men, in another 6 members of his party died.

He, his driver and a security aide locked themselves inside their bulletproof "Suburban" Chevrolet, and refused to comply with the police order. Fortunately Singson was in a celphone conversation with mayors of his province with whom he just had a meeting in a nearby Holiday Inn. He expressed his alarm, and the mayors came to his succor. The police, all poised to shoot, when confronted by the mayors, alleged that Singson violated traffic regulations by using police blinkers on his car, as reported to them by an "anonymous informant." Governor Singson has been going in and out of Malacañang with police blinkers for the last two years and was never challenged. For a minor traffic violation, he was accosted by three cars full of heavily armed men at about midnight in a deserted street?? The set-up, Chavit claims, was obvious. There was dirty work afoot, no doubt about this, he said. The red car contained professional killers. Governor Chavit Singson alleges that the assassination attempt was the work of Atong Ang, a gambler crony of the President, because he knew too much about the protection racket being perpetrated on the jueteng gambling lords. After the face-off with the mayors, the police retreated. Not trusting anyone, Luis Chavit Singson, asked for asylum and sanctuary in the House of Cardinal Sin, and was welcomed there.

What brought this about? A quarrel over spoils? A double cross? A deadly rivalry for the favor of the President? A fight over turf?   It seems that Governor Chavit Singson, a former congressman from Ilocos Sur, is a *compadreng bu-o* of the President, a friend from way back-when, a political supporter, *ka mahjongg-an*, a crony and a member of the President's inner circle and midnight cabinet – real close to President Erap Estrada. He claims that he was asked to be the collector of jueteng protection money for the powers-that-be, and he was that for several years.

Then suddenly Bingo 2 was advocated as a legal substitute for the illegal jueteng operation. Another crony was appointed as a consultant to the Pagcor (which is the legal operator of gambling in the Philippines). As consultant earning P500,000 a day, Atong Ang was able to set up Bingo 2 operations all over the Philippines. Bingo 2 differs little from the jueteng it displaced – it is the same "juego" once played by Rizal and Bonifacio in the 1800s. Bingo 2 and jueteng use the same gambling methods, the same operators, same players, same *cobradores*, same *sumadores*, and same revenue but which now goes to different recipients. This time it is collected 100 percent by Atong Ang, then 23 percent of the revenue is given to the Pagcor.

Two aspects seem anomalous. Why should a "consultant," Atong Ang, be a contractor too, through a company called Prominent Marketing Consultancy – it seems a conflict of interest situation. Why should Atong Ang do the collecting from Bingo 2 operators, later giving part to Pagcor which is the only entity legally entitle to do so. It looks really anomalous.

Part 2. Is Chavit Singson telling a lie or the truth??
According to Chavit Singson, he has no quarrel over the fact that Atong Ang assumed the collection of the jueteng protection money, if that is what the powers-that-be wanted. What he resented most was the persistent rumor that he had been skimming the money he once collected, a rumor that expelled him from favor; and most of all the fact that the jueteng protection racket in his province Ilocos Sur was entrusted to his political enemies, and the provincial police command friendly to him was replaced with those friendly with his rivals.

According to Chavit Singson, this was the last straw. Ilocos Sur is his turf, his kingdom, the source of all his political power, his home and castle. He fought the Crisologos for his place in the sun, no political leader will ever countenance the invasion of his constituency. So he confronted Atong Ang, "Itigil mo ito, o ibulgar kita." Ang laughed, he knows that if Chavit squeals, both of them will probably go to jail, "Sorry, utos ng boss." Chavit went to the boss who denied having given the order. So he went to the chief of the National Police and asked why the were the police command in Ilocos Sur replaced? The chief answered, "Utos ni boss, eh" Chavit knew then that he was a marked man, someone not to be trusted with a secret, a target to be liquidated. And when his car was stopped in a deserted street by three cars full of heavily armed policemen, for a flimsy traffic rule violation, he was convinced his life was in mortal danger.

He called for help from the opposition. At first, they could not believe their ears. "Is this a set-up? Hey listen we do not want to be caught in the crossfire if you and Erap reconcile. We want to be sure you give us solid evidence of wrong-doing before we help you, so that we will not be holding the bag. Do you realize that blowing the whistle on them is blowing the whistle on yourself? Are You willing to go to jail too?"

Chavit's answer is surprising: 'It will be an honor to go to jail as long as Atong Ang and the rest will be with me." But then the opposition leaders asked: "Why should we make a hero out of this wastrel, this squealer, this canary?" And the answer is that the important thing is not the singer, not the song, not the messenger but the message. What Chavit Singson has to say, the evidence presents is the all-important thing. Will it be more credible than the counter allegations of his enemies?

For years, rumors of malfeance in high office, and the excellent exposes by investigative journalists have failed to produce enough evidence to stand up in court or in impeachment proceedings. What was needed was a "smoking gun" and a living breathing witness who can say, "I was there. I saw him do it." And for the opposition leaders, singer and the song are heaven-sent, specially since the economy is sinking fast, the peso and stock-market prices plunging to new lows, the fuel prices transportation costs skyrocketing, and the mid-term election is coming in the middle of next year.

And so sworn statements were made by Governor Luis "Chavit Singson, written proofs and tape recordings attached, and arrangements were made with the media, especially the foreign correspondents to get advanced copies of the same.

Chavit was given sanctuary and refuge, not by the police whom he did not trust, but by Jaime Cardinal Sin himself.

Part 3. For Erap, the situation was desperate but not hopeless

The nation has been plunged into a political and economic crisis by the jueteng scandal. The situation is desperate but not hopeless.

Majority of those polled by the TV and radio stations, mostly residing in Manila, from 60 to 90 percent, are demanding the resignation of President Erap Estrada. But these are not random samples, these are unscientific surveys covering middle class homes with phones. The national surveys of Pulse Asia and Social Weather Station show that most Filipinos, especially to the lower DE class are in favor of Erap. It is not yet hopeless, Mr. President.

Most civic organizations and militant NGOs are organizing rallies and demonstrations for the ouster of Erap and the boycott of crony businessmen. Even the American officialdom and their intelligence agencies are taking an active interest and role in the crisis, getting assurances from Vice President Gloria Macapagal Arroyo that in case she takes over, she will give priority to the problem of China. But the Big Businessmen of the Philippines Incorporated and the most of the movie actors and television hosts advise the militants to cool it and not rock the boat, "katahimikan" is the buzz word of Cuya Germs Moreno.

Cardinal Sin wants Erap to resign, Cory Aquino gives him two options: resign or take a leave of absence while the investigation and impeachment proceedings are going on. Erap accuses his accusers of plotting a coup, predicting a rash of bombings and riots, and not ruling out declaring a state of emergency to restore peace and order. Erap is not expected to resign. Impeachment proceedings will not prosper because he has absolute control of the House and the Senate at the moment. In the long run, it is doubtful if he can keep 73 out of 220 greedy congressmen happy enough to be on his side..

But a crisis of confidence puts his administration in a precarious position. The plunge of the peso and the spiraling price of fuel is fast pushing the country to the edge of disaster.

The refusal of IMF to release the last tranche of $310 million loan to the Philippines is an indication of the international community's perception of the stability of the Estrada Administration. This move certainly will put the unstable peso under heavier pressure. The external financing of budget deficit next year become almost impossible at this point. And the political situation is fast approaching a critical point.

The expose of Governor Chavit Singson against the President has thrown the country into a political crisis with outcome uncertain at this point in time. The expose comes at a particular challenging time for the President as de-stabilizing economic forces converge at the same time on our nation:

The critics of the President charge that this convergence of events is a natural consequence of corruption and incompetence of his crisis-prone administration which reacts to events rather than acts on its own initiative to control events. The middle class ABC economic sectors most affected by the prevalent economic conditions are now galvanized around the issue of jueteng and are demanding that the President resign or go on leave while the investigation of his alleged malfeasance goes on.   But the President refuses to resign and is calling on his political allies, movie celebrities and the DE economic classes for support.

Part 4. Crisis moving fast to its denouement

Like a speeding train without brakes, like a toboggan on a steep slope, the mounting economic and political crisis is fast moving to its denouement. What is likely to happen? Snap election, resignation, leave of absence, impeachment – all are unlikely to occur, seeing that President Erap Estrada is determined to finish his term as part of his mandate upon his election with the biggest electoral victory in history. Impeachment may be an option, in case the heat of controversy becomes too much to bear. But the House of Representatives are a coven of yes-men and prostitutes, they are for sale and they have been already been bought for such a cheap price. Except for a few – Joker Arroyo and the Spice Boys – the Lower House is composed of clowns, morons, crooks, traitors, and criminally insane – child molesters, rapists, gun runners, electoral cheats, murderers, most of whom belong behind bars more than within the halls of the legislature.

I have a feeling that the controversy will be resolved, not politically, not constitutionally, but extra-judicially on the streets. The demonstrations, both pro and con, are spreading to the provinces, at first in 6 cities, then 11 cities and at this writing 18 cities. When or if the army is called out to restore order, then a wild card will come into play. We know that the loyalty of the generals and the colonels are with President Erap Estrada, but how about the majors, captains and the lieutenants and the ordinary soldiers who actually hold the guns. To whom will their guns be pointed?

Now Gloria comes out to unify the opposition, amidst suspicions that she is nothing but an opportunist. The opposition is certainly not united behind her; third force Senator Sergio Osmeña and Senator Raul Roco feel she is not worthy of the support of those who were in opposition to Erap Estrada long before she was. Her first statement that she alone has the calmness and sobriety to stand above the fray and plan for the future did not sit well with the NGOs manning the street barricades. Her next statement that she is not asking Erap to resign because it is self serving, impressed lawyers like Enrique Belo, but it enraged the street parliamentarians.

Fortunately she subsequently called for the resignation of Erap, and made the headlines, although the NGOs, especially the left-of-center, swore that they will oppose her taking over if Erap resigns. But Gloria seems to be making the right moves, taking the initiative to get the Lakas party behind her, and planning a shadow cabinet and a plan for the first 100 days of her presidency, just in case it does happen. By being more militant in her demands, she is also gaining some respect among the street parliamentarians.

Her greatest advantage in the bid for opposition leadership is the fact that according to the constitution, she is the legitimate successor to Erap. But no way can she ever assume the presidency if the constitution is followed. Erap refused to consider resignation, a leave of absence or a snap election. And impeachment and conviction is impossible with Erap's domination of the Congress and the Senate.

The only way Erap will leave the presidency is by street rioting and military take-over, precisely maneuvered by those who at present do not recognize Gloria's leadership, and resent her taking from them the fruits of their labor.

Part 5. God did his part

Jaime Cardinal Sin once admonished us "We can only do so much. Let God do His part." And God did His Part. He moved the Congress to elect Manny Villar as the Speaker who subsequently used his influence to impeach President Erap Estrada. And the scene shifted to the Senate where Chief Justice Hilario Davide became the Chairman of the Senate body to conduct the Impeachment Trial.   Like manna from heaven, corroborating evidence came in the wake of Chavit Singson's accusations in the persons of Yolanda Ricaforte, Emma Lim, Malou Itchon, and Delia Rajas testifying on the paper trail of the jueteng and excise tax money delivered to Erap Estrada. Like manna from heaven came the checks in the name of Jose Velarde and the secret accounts that point to ill-gotten gains, courtesy of witness Clarissa Ocampo, even though it was declared irrelevant and immaterial by vote of 11 senators who voted against the opening of Envelop # 2. With the walkout of the prosecution panel, a constitutional crisis loomed.

Trust Erap Estrada to do the wrong thing and help God to do his job. First, gone is the humility, the contrition and the desire to make up, with which he met the accusations, and its place are threats against the witnesses and against critics who pass judgment on him. Second is the emergence of a shit list of those upon whom the administration wishes to vent its vengeance -- many businessmen and members of the media, including me whose contract with Channel 9 was canceled upon orders from above. And third is the arrogance and gloating that mocked us in our hour of defeat and despair. This gloating hour is to be remembered, filed away in some unwashed corner of the brain, if such there be, to await a better time if such can possibly come.

The obnoxious performance of the dancing lady Senator Tessie Oreta after the 11 Senators voted, was the turning point, the moment of truth. In his Palace at Villa San Miguel, Jaime Cardinal Sin saw this woman dancing, "I pity her, I pity her! I could not sleep. So I called you here to share my waking hours." He took to the radio to call the people back to Edsa. Thousands of citizens came to Edsa, summoned by an avalanche of text messages on the cellphone. They came honking their car horns, beating drums and kitchen utensils. On the TV appeared Erap spokesmen Ernesto Maceda who plucks his eyebrows, gloating, yes gloating, and telling us that the street demonstration will die down after five days as Erap's regime assumes the full authority to govern us. Above all the swaggering, bullying womanizer, gambler, thief and liar who has lost the moral ascendancy to govern us -- has driven us back to Edsa, together with our children who have become old enough and are only too glad to participate in another moment of historic decision.

In Room 716 of the Makati Medical Center, sat a 50-year-old-man afflicted with mumps, for God's sake, mumps, a disease he should have contracted in childhood. His name is Pastor "Boy" Saycon who is neither a pastor, nor a boy, nor a psycho. And he is one of the characters who triggered the anti Erap movement and the Edsa II revolt. I saw him was in the company of my cousin Antonio Oppen in the afternoon of January 18. Sitting on his bed, he had before him four cellphones and one transceiver with scramblers continuously ringing. He answered each in turn, barking orders, seeking advice, talking to politicians and army generals, cajoling, appealing, advising, doing the things he does best, calling on his network of various diverse segments, often conflicting, to get their act together to achieve a common goal. He sat through the Edsa revolt of January 19, glued to the television set near bed, practically forgotten, and saw everyone else mount the stage at Edsa and claim credit for many things than this man had done.

Then God's miracle happened. The Erap government collapsed completely with a million citizens screaming for him to resign at Edsa, most of his cabinet members (Jose Pardo, Felipe Medalla, Andrew Gonzalez, Alfredo Lim) resigning, and the armed forces from DND Secretary Mercado to the Chief of Staff and service commanders capitulating. Erap Estrada's crooked cronies, bribed supporters and highly paid lawyers scurried like rats leaving a sinking ship to Hong Kong, the United States and elsewhere to escape the collective wrath of the Filipino and enjoy their ill-gotten gains, which they demanded and received up front because they did not trust their untrustworthy leader President Erap Estrada..

Joy and Sorrow

At this writing, Gloria Macapagal Arroyo took her oath as the 14th President of the Republic of the Philippines.
October 9, 2000 to January 24, 2001, Philippine Post

ooooo

Chapter Five: YANKEE, GO HOME

Part 1. Dug-out Dog and the double cross

Tomorrow is the 57th anniversary of the Fall of Bataan (April 9, 1942), and after Holy Week, we remember the passion and death of the Fil-American forces during the early part of World War II. We remember because in the wake of the bases question and the new Visiting Forces Agreement signed with the Americans, we experience the same rhetoric from Americans, echoes of President Roosevelt's message that American convoys are on their way across the Pacific to rescue us from the Japs. The rhetoric contrasts with the reality.

The reality of deceit and betrayal, of promises broken -- of the sabotage of our efforts to industrialize, keeping us a vegetable garden to an industrial estate -- of the arrogance of white trash passing judgment on his brown brothers -- of crimes unpunished, of women and children abused, of drugs, prostitution and venereal diseases -- throughout our entire history as a nation, again rears their ugly heads.

For years, Americans used Bataan and Corregidor as trigger words to induce us into a hypnotic state of colonial subservience. For years they made us believe that they fought for us, when all the time we were fighting for them, under their command and under their flag, to make the world safe for their democracy. That's more than the Malays, Indons and the Vietnamese did for their colonial masters.

President Quezon knew early in 1942 that Americans had betrayed us. In *The Rising Sun*, John Toland narrates:

"On Corregidor, Quezon in his wheel chair listened in mounting fury as Roosevelt told a radio audience how thousands of aircraft would soon be on the way to the battlefront -- Europe. Quezon pointed to smoke rising from the mainland. "For 30 years I have worked and hoped for my people. Now they burn and die for a flag that could not protect them. *Por Dios y todos los santos!* I cannot stand this constant reference to England, to Europe.

"Where are the planes this *sin verguenza* (scoundrel) is boasting of? How American to writhe in anguish at the fate of a distant cousin while a daughter is being raped in the backroom!"

Douglas MacArthur was no hero to his men either. During the battle of Bataan, Gen. MacArthur stayed in the tunnels of

Corregidor, while his soldiers in Bataan scornfully called him "Dug-out Doug" and sang to the tune of the *Battle Hymn of the Republic*: "Dug-out Doug MacArthur lies/ A-shakin' on the Rock/ Safe from all the bombers/ And from any sudden shock..."

There is a hint of blackmail in the story that Quezon sent instructions to deposit $500,000 to the personal account of MacArthur from Philippine funds in the USA, just before both of them left for Australia, with a megalomanic promise to the Filipino people, "I shall return."

Late in 1944, the US Joint Chiefs of Staff decided to bypass Luzon (and Manila) and leapfrog all the way from Leyte to Taiwan. Toland narrates that this would in effect eliminate MacArthur's cherished role as Liberator of the Philippines, and his reply was in keeping with his indignation:

"The Philippines is American territory where 17,000,000 Filipinos remain loyal to the United States. We have a great national obligation to discharge. If the United States should deliberately bypass the Philippines, we would probably suffer loss of prestige among all the peoples of the Far East..." It was of course his own personal prestige that Dug-out Doug was worried about.

"Marshall replied with a forceful admonition 'not to let personal feelings and Philippine politics overshadow his primary objective, the winning of the war... that 'bypassing' was by no means synonymous with abandonment.

George Marshall argued that invading Manila would cause unnecessary loss of Filipino lives -- avoided if the war were brought directly to Taiwan. Dug-out Doug appealed to President Roosevelt who knew full well that the Atom Bomb was getting ready to be deployed against Japan. In spite of this knowledge, President Roosevelt supported General Douglas MacArthur. Dug-out Dog MacArthur wanted his personal glory, to fulfill his vow "I shall return," even if it uselessly caused the death of a million Filipinos, the worst calamity of the war, worse than the Rape of Warsaw. How many loved ones have we Filipinos lost to satisfy MacArthur's megalomania?? President Elpidio Quirino lost his wife and daughter. President Cory Aquino lost the brother of her father, a cousin and a cousin-in-law. My wife got shot and lost her leg.

Yet we consider this asshole Dug-out Dog a hero, naming MacArthur Highway after him. Worse than that, we allowed him and his sidekick Edelstein to interfere in our politics, placed Recto, Laurel and other patriots in jail, and ensured the election of Manuel Roxas who readily signed the military bases agreement and sponsored the parity rights amendment in our constitution to grant the Americans all the business privileges of the Filipino Citizen.

Then MacArthur and his ilk, facing a rejection in the Senate of the infamous Parity Rights Amendment, had the effrontery to cause the ejection of three patriotic Senators including Pepe Diokno's dad, so that Americans may win their parity rights by one lousy vote.

William Manchester observed that on Mt. Natib in Bataan, *Dambana ng Kagitingan* (Altar of Valor) stands as a monument to the dead of World War II. Chiseled letters seem to mock us who lived most of our lives under the sufferance of the CIA and the military, "To live in freedom's light is the right of mankind."

Manchester added, as if to describe the special relations between the Filipino and the American: "Above it stands a crucifix formed of two parallel uprights and two horizon bars. It can only be described as a double cross."
April 8-9, 1999

Part 2. US marines are 'gangsters for capitalism'

AMERICAN marines are called Leathernecks because they once wore a leather strap around their necks to protect them from saber cuts. The marines like the Jesuit "light cavalry," are first to attack, to secure the beach-heads. From the halls of Montezuma to the shores of Tripoli, from Guadalcanal to Iwo Jima, the list is long and Gung Ho!

The Marine Corps founded in 1775 in time to fight in the War of Independence, fought in every war specializing in amphibious operations. With motto Semper Fidelis, the sea-soldier belonged to the smallest and deadliest fighting force in the USA. In the Spanish American War, it had only 75 officers and 2,000 men; at the start of World War I, 511 officers and 13,124 men, growing to 31,824; by the end of World War II, 403,000 men.

Today, marines man the secondary batteries aboard navy ships and guard naval property within the USA. But its big job is to protect American bases and embassies outside of USA, and to do police action in all parts of the world.

During peacetime US marines found themselves the instruments of American imperial policy, in Shanghai in the 1920s, occupying Nicaragua, Panama, Guatemala, Honduras, Mexico many times, and Beirut as late as 1958. No heroism there and many marines felt used and betrayed.

"Like all members of the military profession I never had an original thought," said an American marine general, saying in effect that one does not need any brains to be a good soldier -- just take orders from above and pass the same orders below, "Their's not to reason why, their's but to do or die," as Tennyson wrote in his poem, The Charge of the Light Brigade.

The American is retired Major General Smedley Butler, US Marine Corps, quoted in full here in an article printed in Common Sense magazine November 1935:

I spent 33 years and four months in active military service as a member of our country's most agile military force -- the Marine Corps. I served in all commissioned ranks from Second Lieutenant to Major General. And during that period, I spent most of my time being a high class muscleman for Big Business, for Wall Street and for the bankers. In short, I was a racketeer, a gangster for capitalism.

I suspected I was just part of a racket at the time. Now I am sure of it. Like all members of the military profession I never had an original thought until I left the service. My mental faculties remained in suspended animation while I obeyed the orders of the higher-ups. This is typical with everyone in the military service.

Thus I helped make Mexico and especially Tampico safe for American oil interests in 1914. I helped make Haiti and Cuba a decent place for the National City Bank boys to collect revenues in. I helped in the raping of a half a dozen Central American republics for the benefit of Wall Street.

The record of racketeering is long. I helped purify Nicaragua for the international banking house of Brown Brothers in 1909-12. I brought light to the Dominican Republic for American sugar interests in 1916. In China in 1927 I helped to see to it that Standard Oil went its way unmolested.

During those years, I had, as the boys in the back room would say, a "swell racket." I was rewarded with honors, medals and promotion. Looking back on it, I feel that I might have given Al Capone a few hints. The best he could do was to operate his racket in three city districts. I operated in three continents.

Al Capone is America's most famous gangster, played by Robert de Niro in the movie The Untouchables, the antagonist of Elliot Ness and the FBI. He ran a protection racket, murder for hire, official corruption, and gin smuggling.

This is roughly analogous to what the Americans are doing here in the Philippines and elsewhere.

They run a protection racket, "We are here to protect you from the Russians," ha ha ha.

They offer murder for hire, with their LIC bloodbath doctrine, by which Filipinos are given deadly weapons to murder and mutilate anyone opposed to American bases and business monopolies.

They corrupt our officials, by travel grants, by promises of support for presidential ambitions, to place American interests way above that of our own country.

And they run the equivalent of smuggling and economic sabotage -- by tax-free importation through the bases, and by Import Liberalization.

No wonder Marines feel like gangsters.
May 31, 1988

Part 3. We deserve that pile of SHIT!

The story goes that at the beginning of time, Juan de la Cruz went to God with an unusual request. "My Lord," he said, "give me a country with fertile lands, bountiful seas and rivers, and mountains laden with rich minerals."

And God answered: "Yes, of course, my son. Your wish is granted."

Then Juan de la Cruz said: "Give my country, beautiful beyond all imagination – the bluest of skies, the whitest of clouds, the greenest of forests, golden sunsets and sunrises, and rainbows with the most beautiful kaleidoscope of colors and hues."

"Done, my son, you deserve it," said the Lord. Thus encouraged, Juan de la Cruz asked for more. "Give me women of fair and golden skin, and faces like translucent alabaster stained with rose petals. Let them have eyes that twinkle like newly created stars beneath a canopy of hair cloaked in the blackest of night. Let them be tall and slender, with breasts like twin peaks topped with pink snow, a smile that is as warm and bright as the sun, and soft arms that stretch out in longing, love and passion."

"Whew," the Lord said, "you sure ask for perfection, Johnny. What else do you want?"

Juan waxed eloquent. "Well, Lord, as long as you give me the perfect women, you might as well give me the most perfect of men – men of courage and wisdom, men of vision and industry, men of strength and endurance."

"Done, enough, and be gone, Juan de la Cruz, you already have heaven on earth," said the Lord.

"But, my Lord," protested St. Peter, "if the Philippines is heaven on earth, who will want to go to your heaven up here? It will be empty."

God smiled, and said, "Well, Johnny still does not know what kind of political leaders I will give him. If he did, he will go elsewhere."

"Where?" asked Peter.

God laughed and laughed and laughed till his eyes filled with tears and said, "You remember what happened to Noah's Ark? Never mind the mosquito and the ant, but the elephant and the lion and big animals started to fill the boat with so much heavy manure that Noah's Ark began to sink. Desperately, Noah asked me what to do, and I told him to sail as far west as he can and dump the manure overboard.

"10,000 years later, Christopher Columbus discovered that pile of shit. It is now called America. And that is where Juan de la Cruz will want to go, when he can no longer stand the kind of political leaders I will give him. He deserves that pile of shit."
August, 2017

Part 4. How Multinationals Operate In The Philippines
It is really a surprise and a pleasure to be invited to speak before you today under the auspices of no less than the United States Information Service, but it does put me in the same position I was in when as a candidate for the Senate, I was invited to speak in Ilocos Norte, deep in Marcos country. I was called upon to speak on the economic policies of President Marcos, and I wasted no time and minced no words doing so.... until I saw the men in

the audience somewhat irritated, then exasperated, and finally enraged. One by one the Ilocanos started to take their guns from their waist-bands, and pointed the guns tentatively at the offending speaker.

"I hope you are not going to shoot me!" I exclaimed. One of the leaders stood up and replied, "Mr. Henares, you were invited here to speak, so speak your piece in peace. We are not going to shoot you. But we are going to shoot the man who invited you." And so my dear friends, if I say anything to offend any one of you, please remember that it was Bill DeMyer himself who invited me here. You are free to do with him as you wish, after he pays the bill for this wonderful weekend.

How do multinational corporations operate in the Philippines? It really started with the Treaty of Paris by which the United States claimed sovereignty over the Philippines, and the Payne-Aldrich Act of 1909 by which Free Trade was established between the United States and the Philippines, and tariff barriers were set up against all other countries. These resulted in the entry of American investments in agriculture, extractive industries and trading companies catering to the needs of the American economy by exporting raw materials and importing finished products; the supremacy of American companies with respect to their technological equals and natural competitors from Europe and Japan; the rise of an indigenous landed aristocracy in the Philippines, supplying sugar, copra and minerals; a one-way free trade by which the United States exported any and all products in unlimited quantities to the Philippines, while imposing quotas and duties on our major exports. In short, this era was characterized by a colonial plantation-type import-export economy dominated by American business interests. It was the time when the American Chamber of Commerce of the Philippines actively opposed Philippine Independence, issuing at least 3 times a pamphlet widely distributed in the United States which said, and we quote: "We (Americans) are here by right, we are here by conquest and we have a title by conquest, and a title by purchase. We are here as possessors and we are here as sovereigns; we are here as owners and controllers of sovereignty."

Forced to initiate manufacturing operations during the era of Import and Exchange Controls, American companies nevertheless held on to their dominant status by virtue of "parity rights" granted by the Bell Trade Act and the Laurel Langley Agreement. Thus did American companies continue to preempt the most profitable businesses in the Philippines. In 1973, Professor Vicente Valdepeñas of the Ateneo University (who is now Deputy Minister of Trade) stated that in the wholesale and retail trade, in mining sectors and in four industry groups, foreign controlled companies predominate. In the wholesale trade foreign operators accounted for 60.7% of the output and 59.4% of the input. In Industry they accounted for 52.1% of metal products; 57.6% of rubber products; 68.9% of chemicals and chemical products; and 100% of petroleum and coal products.

PROFITABILITY AND GREED

How profitable are American companies today? and what do they do with their profits? I cite two studies available today: (1) The Bantegui Report of 1968, which compiled data on 108 out of a total of 157 registered American companies operating in the Philippines over a period of ten years from 1956 to 1965, roughly covering the period of Control and Decontrol, and (2) The study of the Technology Resource Center dated 1978, in which I participated, covering the operations of a representative group of 31 foreign companies, mostly American, over a period of 5 years from 1971 to 1976, roughly covering the first years of Martial Law.

According to the Bantegui Report:

(1) Out of a paid-up capital of $74.2 million in 1956, American companies generated $389.3 million in profits in ten years, 524.66% in ten years, or an average of 52.5% per year on original capital.

(2) Of these $389.3 million profit, $369.0 million or 95% was remitted back to the parent company and a measly 5% reinvested in the local company.

According to the TRC report:

(1) Out of the paid in capital of P380.7 million at the end of 1971, the foreign companies generated P1,159.6 million profit or 305% in 5 years, or an average of 60.15% per year original paid-in capital. Original paid-in capital in this case refers to the capital stock" outstanding at the end of 1971, which is equivalent to original investment and re-investments of previous years.

(2) Of this P1,159.6 million profit P537.7 million or 46% was given out as cash dividends.

(3) The biggest profit-making firms are 3M Philippines, which averaged 351.8% profit per year on original paid in capital; Rohm & Haas Philippines, 319% per year; and Pepsi Cola Far East Trade, 202.2% profit per year.

(4) Of those who declared cash dividends, the biggest are: Pepsi Cola Far East Trade, which declared cash dividends exceeding its profits, P40.98 million cash dividends out of profits totalling only P36.98 million, sending to the parent company 110% of profits; Globe Mackay Cable & Radio, which declared cash dividends of P45.78 million out of P55.44 million profit, or 82% of profits; Ford Philip- pines, which declared P1.19 million cash dividends even as it incurred a loss of P7.88 million; and Weyerhauser Phil. Inc which declared cash dividends also exceeding its prof- its, P36.1 million cash dividends out of only P30.9 million profit, or 116% of profits.

SOURCE OF CAPITAL: DOMESTIC RESOURCES

From the end of World War II, a whole generation of national leaders and economic planners, specially of developing countries, have proceeded on the assumption that foreign investment is the *sine-qua-non* in the economic development of nations. A whole mass of US-inspired propaganda conspired to convince the rest of the world that foreign investment holds forth three advantages that may accrue to the host country: managerial know-how, technology, and above all, large amounts of new capital.

It became fairly obvious as the years went by that managerial know-how can be learned, and technology can be bought and that the only real advantage to be derived from foreign investment is that it will bring into the host country the enormous capital needed but sadly lacking.

Soon thereafter, during the 1960's, the "Decade of Development" as decreed by the United Nations, Third World nations in their development plans were beginning to perceive that the contribution of foreign direct investment was minimal. For instance, the first Five Year Socio-Economic Program during the Macapagal Administration showed that of the total capital expenditure needed, only a measly 3% can be contributed by direct foreign investment, 11% by foreign loans, and fully 88% by local sources.

Not only that, it was increasing apparent that foreign corporations were bringing into the host country a minimal amount of capital and raising an inordinately large portion of their capital requirements from local sources, thus depriving local entrepreneurs access to national savings.

In Latin America, where there is an accumulated history of American direct investments dating back to the turn of the century, a United Nations study by Fernando Fajnzylber showed that U.S.-based multinationals financed 83% of their Latin American investments from reinvested profits and domestic borrowings, so that only 17% therefore represents a real transfer of capital from the United States to the poor countries of Latin America.

In the Philippines, when the effects of the Laurel Langley Agreement came up for study, a NEC report by B. G. Bantegui on 108 American corporations doing business in the Philippines, covering a ten year period from 1956 to 1965, showed that out of a total capital expenditure of $489.7 million, fully 88% or $431.1 million was generated from local sources.

The TRC study covering 31 foreign companies during a 5 year period from 1971 to 1976, roughly the Martial Law period, shows the following:

(1) At the end of 1971, they had total assets of P2,077.8 million, which was financed by local sources to the extent of 75%, or P1,553.5 million.

(2) During the intervening period from 1971 to 1976, their total assets increased by P2,552.9 million, which was financed by local sources to the extent of 74%, or P1,888.9 million. The most controversial of the corporations are the following:

(3) Ford Philippines, which financed its increase in assets (P123.3 million) with local borrowings of P144.3 million, or 110% of the value of the assets (local borrowings were also used to finance operating deficits and to repay foreign loans);

(4) Carnation Philippines which financed an increase in assets of P40.9 million through local borrowings of P36.6 million (90% of the assets);

(5) Findlay Miller Timber Co., which financed P17.9 million increase in assets with local borrowings of P23.3 million or 130% of the increase in assets (local borrowings were also used to pay foreign loans);

(6) Globe Mackay Cable & Radio which secured from local sources P52.9 million or 106% of the value of the increase in assets P50.1 million).

IMPACT ON BALANCE OF PAYMENTS

The most horrifying fact about foreign multinationals is their collective impact on the host country's balance of payments position. Every year, they bring in new investments, foreign loans and credits; at the same time, they also bring out profit remittances, amortization of loans, payments for royalties and interests, and withdrawal of investments. "Investment Income" as categorized in balance of payments tables, which sums up interest payments and profit remittances derived from investments of multinational corporations, is pointedly placed in "Current Accounts" to emphasize the sanctity and priority attached to it by the International Monetary Fund.

During the period from 1949 to 1960, a Central Bank report indicated that there was an Outflow of $223 million and an Inflow of $16.2 million, or $14 going out for every $1 coming in.

From 1956 to 1965, according to the Bantegui Report, 108 American companies took out $386.2 million while bringing in $58.6 million, or $6.50 going out for every dollar brought in.

From 1964 to 1971, Central Bank statistics indicated an Outflow of $3,017.58 million and an Inflow of $549.32 million, or $5.49 going out for every dollar coming in.

From 1971 to 1976, according to the TRC report, 30 foreign companies sent out P656.76 million, while bringing in from abroad P98.03 million, or in dollar terms, $6.70 going out for every dollar coming in.

This unremitting drain on foreign exchange reserves is bad enough, but it does not even include the effects of the pernicious and widespread practice of "transfer pricing" by which exports are undervalued and imports are overvalued in transactions between subsidiaries and their parent companies, in order to save on taxes paid in the host country or merely to effect illegal remittances of profits. A variation often used and even more favored is to ship underpriced exports and overpriced imports to a tax-free port such as Hong Kong or the Bahamas (known as tax havens), and to re-export the goods at their normal value or even at an inflated price to another subsidiary in the country where they are to be sold.

Company manuals on how to run multinational corporations are filled with detailed instructions on intra-company transfers to maximize the global profits of the parent company.

Transfer pricing, which is an open secret among multinationals in the Philippines, is a ruthless act of exploitation of the poor nations of the world who suffer on two counts: (1) they lose needed tax revenue owing to understated income, and (2) they lose valuable foreign exchange through undervalued exports and overvalued imports.

The effect of transfer pricing shows up in the ever widening gap between imports and exports by underdeveloped countries. Prices for raw material exports, specially minerals and agricultural products, decline or are frozen; prices of finished goods imports are ever spiraling. Balance-of-trade statistics of underdeveloped nations seem perpetually in chronic deficit. Many factors contribute to this deficit, of course, and transfer pricing is a major contributor. But it is, under present conditions, almost impossible to quantify the amount of transfer pricing. One can only pinpoint examples.

In the Philippines, a Senate Committee found that Esso Philippines was buying oil from its subsidiaries at $1.74 per barrel at the time the published price ranged from 99 cents to $1.34 per barrel.

Esteban Bautista of the U.P. Law Center testified that the local subsidiary of Bristol/Mead Johnson bought from its mother company Ampicillin at prices from $177.98 to $242.99 per kilo, and a local subsidiary of Beecham bought he same drug from its parent company for $251.00 per kilo. On the other hand, a local firm, Doctors Pharmaceuticals bought from other sources the same drug at prices as low as $91.40 per kilo, almost one third of the transfer prices of multinational corporations.

Philippine Packing Corp. (Del Monte) persists in transshipping its exports through Hong Kong; National City Bank of New York gets a lot of its loans through Hong Kong, giving rise to the suspicion that the Bank is "parking" its funds at a higher rate of interest to avoid taxes, as was exposed in the January 1983 issue of Fortune. All these and many more, and so on *ad nauseaum*.

POLITICAL ABUSE AND GUN-BOAT DIPLOMACY

For centuries, conquerors dreamed of world domination by force of arms. None ever succeeded for any length of time. Only the Catholic Church with no armies of its own ever succeeded to some degree, offering a faith that embraced all nations, but today its power is on the wane. Today, the managers of multinational corporations proclaim that where conquest and faith have failed, Free Enterprise will succeed. With the skills and resources to straddle the earth, the Multinational has been described as the New World Force, a Transcendental Unity, a Wave of the Future, an instrument for world development, the only force for peace, the most powerful agent for the internationalization of human society, the "prologue to a new world symphony".

Indeed, the sheer size and power of multinational corporations stagger the imagination. If we compare the annual sales of the largest corporations with the gross na- tional product (GNP) of countries, as Lester Brown has done in his "Interdependence of Nations" we find that General Motors is larger than Switzerland, is larger than South Africa, and is six times larger than the Philippines.

Power corrupts, and the multinational is no exception. American business interests were behind the fight for and against our Independence, and set the terms for our eventual liberation from American colonialism, saddling our economy with Free Trade and American Parity Rights for most of our national existence. American multinationals were behind the successful attempt to emasculate the Filipino First policy and the Retail Trade Nationalization Law; the non-passage of the Anti-Trust Act and the Equal Pay for Equal Work legislation in our Congress; the sabotage of the integrated steel industry; the entry of the infamous United Fruit Co. into the Philippines and the leasing of the Davao Penal Colony lands under conditions patently unconstitutional; the grant of third frequency rights to Pan-Am and Northwest Airlines without corresponding concessions to our own flag carrier; the extension of the franchises of Globe-Mackay and RCA up to the year 2015 A.D., thus putting Philippine communications with the outside world, and therefore the security of our nation, in the hands of Americans till the next century. The United States government, the IMF and the World Bank, the GATT, the Paris Club of industrialized nations, the Patent Convention, the

Copyright Union, the International Chamber of Commerce, the Trilateral Commission, and the corrupt economic elite in every poor country serve the interests of the Multinationals.

Today we are witnessing the World Bank with its "structural adjustment loans" (unacceptable anywhere except in the Philippines) actually forcing our government to dismantle protective tariffs at the time when industrialized nations are setting up barriers to protect their industries; to raise interest rates and devalue our currency; to revert back to a colonial plantation-type import-export cottage-industry economy; to promote concentrated economic power in our banking system that will never be countenanced in the United States itself; to tamper with our educational system so as to condition the minds of our youth to the exploitation by foreigners of our resources. And all for the benefit of Multinational Corporations!

A TYPICAL CASE: FORD PHILIPPINES

How do multinational corporations operate in the Philippines? To most Filipinos, the most typical case is that of Ford Philippines, although in my book for sheer gall and cheek, Ford is hard to beat. But it is interesting to see how American pressure can inveigle the Philippine government into giving special advantages to an American company.

When the Philippine government embarked on the establishment of a Progressive Car Manufacturing Program, it announced that only FOUR firms will be selected on the basis of certain criteria. Ford Philippines was not among those qualified, so the government was persuaded to increase the participating firms to FIVE, solely to accommodate Ford.

While the government secretly contemplated banning the manufacture of all but four-cylinder cars, Ford somehow found out about it. Ford then asked for and was given an ADVANCE on its quarterly allocations that permitted it to bring in six-cylinder LTD's and Custom models. Shortly thereafter the ban went into effect, leaving Ford with a monopoly of six-cylinder cars. No other competing firm was given advance allocations.

In a speech before the 2nd Businessmen's Conference, I exposed the fact that foreign corporations, especially American, invested a minimal amount in the Philippines and financed their operations by local borrowings. This contradicted the conventional wisdom that foreign investments brought in their own capital. As an example, I cited Ford Philippines which had a paid-up capital of P1.3 million in 1975, and proceeded to borrow P168.6 million from local sources to finance its operations. With unmitigated gall, Ford also managed to secure authority to issue short term commercial papers for P232.95 million more! Ford then incurred losses that reduced its equity to a Capital Deficit of P4.8 million, at the time Delta Motors Corp. and DMG Motors accumulated a Capital Surplus of P11 million each. No one can tell whether this is because Ford is an inefficient producer, or that it has been overpricing its CKD parts to transfer profits abroad.

The expose' of Ford's duplicity and greed triggered a government investigation and a decision to force foreign corporations to adhere to a 60:40 debt-to-equity ratio. To everybody's surprise, Ford Philippines whose case started the scandal, sought and was given a not so temporary delay in the implementation of this order. Needless to say, most every other firm had to comply.

In spite of the vehement protests of the Council for Energy Conservation headed by no less than Assemblyman Emilio Abello, the Board of Investments promulgated a tailor-made regulation allowing the importation of Ford Granada six-cylinder cars as a special privilege granted to Ford for exporting Stamped Body parts.

Like Ford the Corporate Dracula.... that is how Multinational Corporations operate in the Philippines.

I thank you.

USIS 13th Tagaytay Seminar, February 27, 1983

Part 5. On Virata And The World Bank

This is not to imply that Prime Minister Cesar Virata is a "tool of the IMF and the World Bank", because he is not. His loyalty to the President and to the Republic, as well as his competence and honesty, must remain unquestioned. He is a friend, and between friends, there is room for an honest difference of opinion.

Minister Virata said in his press conference yesterday that "if borrowing means losing sovereignty, then one must not borrow", meaning that we cannot borrow from the IMF and the World Bank if we are not willing to meet all their conditions, however repugnant to our national dignity and an affront to our sovereignty.

If Minister Virata and his technocrats are to be faulted at all, it is that they were not able to bargain effectively for conditions consistent with our national sovereignty, for the Philippines accepted conditions no other self-respecting nation would accept. I am referring mainly to the "Structural Adjustment Loans" imposed upon us by the World Bank.

In contrast to the traditional project loan, the Structural Adjustment Loan (SAL) is a program loan, a new type of loan that is meant to cover an entire economic sector, such as agriculture, industry, banking or energy. Unlike a project loan that is given on the basis of the economic viability of such projects as hydro-electric dams or irrigation systems, the SAL is given only after a thorough overhaul of all government policies within the economic sector. It is the World Bank bureaucrat's dream come true, for it formalized World Bank surveillance and control over a wide swath of the economy.

It is not surprising then that the SAL was viewed with suspicion and repugnance by so many borrowing countries that as of 1980, only four countries, Kenya, Turkey, Bolivia, and the Philippines, were willing to accept the conditions that came with the loan. Other nations in worse financial straits, such as India, Mexico, Brazil and Argentina, were able to borrow World Bank funds without the humiliation of having to surrender the right to pursue their own economic priorities.

Nowhere else, neither in Turkey or Bolivia or Kenya has the World Bank secured the complete and unquestioning acceptance by the national leaders of the SAL than in the Philippines, where the World Bank/IMF economic missions were welcomed into every sector of our national economy, there to effect drastic and irreversible changes in our priorities that are, in the opinion of many, inimical to the interest of the Filipino people.

In other words, as far as the World Bank is concerned, the Philippines is a very special case, a guinea pig to test the validity of the World Bank policies, a Model to show off to the rest of the unbelieving Third World. Why the Philippines, and not some other country?

Only in the Philippines does the World Bank encounter technocrat leaders who are either pliant and obedient, or true believers in the role of the IMF and the World Bank as the Messiah of economic progress.

What are the conditions imposed by the World Bank on the Philippines that it could not impose on other nations?

First, the Banking Sector. The WB Financial Mission "recommendations" resulted in an upheaval that brought Foreign Banks as partners into the ownership and management of most of our banks, and then forced them into mergers and consolidations to comply with the requirements for Unibanking. Unibanks constitute concentrations of economic power with the right to invest directly in industrial corporations... something that is considered dangerous and undesirable in the United States itself. Yet it is done in the Philippines because the fewer and larger the banks are, and the more the participation of foreign bankers, the easier to control them and make them serve the financial needs of multinational corporations. And to ice the cake, foreign banks are now allowed to operate Offshore Banking Units, which now demand more privileges to further erode the position of Filipino bankers.

In the field of Monetary Policy, the WB Financial Mission was able to force our government to pursue a policy of Tight Credit, high interest rates, higher taxes, full convertibility of currency, floating exchange rate tantamount to devaluation, access of Multinational Corporations to domestic resources in competition with Filipino borrowers, unrestricted profit remittances, and capital repatriation by foreigners.

Most appalling was the abdication of the Central Bank with the creation of an autonomous unit within the CB, called the "Apex Development Finance Unit" (ADFU) under the direct control of the World Bank. The ADFU was originally created to administer the WB APEX loans for.the financing of "labor intensive" and "export oriented" projects. Upon the insistence of the WB, this ADFU now serves as a beachhead from which the World Bank could expand to directly control most of the Philippines' external borrowing policies. For this autonomous unit, this WB within the CB, will now administer not only WB loans, but also Asian Development Bank loans and funds from other sources, including foreign commercial banks.

In the field of Industrialization, the World Bank Industrial Mission pressured the Philippine government into a complete reversal of policy, designed primarily to destroy the industrial middle class, negate development based on production for domestic consumption, and assign the Philippines to the role of a Sweatshop in the world economy, for the benefit of multinational corporations, and advanced industrial nations.

First to go were all strictures on foreign corporations including a redefinition of retail trade, the right to lease lands in perpetuity, the right to exploit natural resources under contract, the right to engage in all businesses in competition with Filipinos, the right to borrow from domestic resources, to remit profits and repatriate capital without restrictions.

Second was the "liberalization of import restrictions" which involved dismantling CB categories that discriminate between necessary and unnecessary imports, between industrial and consumer products, between necessities and luxuries. It also involved the dismantling of the entire system of Tariff Protection, leaving our industries helpless against the unfair competition of subsidized foreign imports. The World Bank bluntly told our government in its "Philippines: Prospects and Priorities Report", page 6: "for the future, it should be the government's policy to gradually remove the quantitative restrictions (on imports), to restructure and lower tariff levels, and to delete the protective element from other fiscal and other monetary policies."

Most devastating of all, is the shift from a policy of self-reliance based on production for domestic consumption to a policy to promote "labor-intensive, export-oriented industries" geared to fill the needs of advanced countries and totally dependent on fiercely competitive and unstable fickle markets absolutely beyond our control. One of the cruel jokes of the WB is its project to modernize the Textile industry, to serve an export market that is already severely curtailed by quotas imposed by industrialized nations.

What are the results of the IMF/World Bank impositions on the economy of the Philippines? An accelerated rate of bankruptcies among our industrial and commercial firms due to tight credit, high rates of interest, unfair competition of foreign goods, peso devaluation and spiraling costs, a high rate of unemployment, along with decrease in real wages due to inflation, strike ban, and wage restraints designed to attract foreigners to our "high skilled, low cost labor". And a permanent trade balance deficit due to inability to limit imports of non-essentials and products that compete with locally manufactured goods, a permanent balance of payments deficit due to unrestricted outflow of foreign profits, restricted market for our low value-added WB-aided exports, and a burgeoning trade deficit, while the death of our industries foreshadow a time when we cannot even meet the basic needs of our population.

Even the field of Education was not spared. A World Bank Mission has recently prepared guide-lines for our textbooks and educational curriculum, emphasizing the beneficent role of foreign corporations and industrial nations in the economic development of the Philippines, a brainwashing that is uncalled for, and adds insult to injury.

It is one thing to say that our Technocrat leaders were blackmailed and outwitted by the World Bank into making the Philippines the Great Experiment to relegate the Third World into a subsidiary role in a world economy dominated by the Imperial Powers. It is quite another thing to realize that our Technocrat leaders actually believe in the divine rights of advanced nations, and the WB/IMF; that they being obedient and subservient because they are true believers in the role of the IMF and the World Bank as the Messiah of economic progress. They fancy themselves as citizens of the world, with a vision of the world economy as a Global Market served by multinational corporations, motivated by the logic of profit. If the latter is true, they have no business being officials of the Philippine Republic. They should serve in the IMF, World Bank, the GATT or the United Nations.

But if they choose to serve the Filipino People who pay their salaries, then they must be partisan in their actuations. They must promote and protect and defend the interests of Filipinos, in the same way American officials promote and protect and defend the interests of American citizens. American officials restrict the entry into their market of our sugar, coconut oil, mahogany, textiles, and many of our major export products, just as they restrict the imports of Japanese cars and TV sets, solely to protect the hard-pressed American industries. Our technocrats can do no less to make sure that World Bank (which is controlled by the US by virtue being its largest shareholder, and mandated by US law to obey US officials) be treated as a surrogate of the USA, so that multinational corporations and industrial nations do not wax fat on the bones of

bankrupt Filipino firms and on the hunger and suffering of the Filipino people.
A Press Statement dated May 6, 1983

Part 6. Robert Marx given monopoly of galleon salvage
In 1944 French explorer Jacques Costeau invented the Self Contained Underwater Breathing Apparatus (initials: scuba), and a new world opened up. Freed from diving gear with leaden shoes, pressure suit and an umbilical cord of air to the surface, man could now roam the deep of ocean like a fish, free from gravity like a man in space.

My son Atom at the age of 12 was the youngest certified scuba diver of his time, so was my daughter Juno at 11, and later Rosanna at 10 -- all because we had a swimming pool American and Filipino scuba divers were free to use for formal training.

Allan Staley, Paul Rosenberg; Henry Leung who took Atom to Iloilo and Palawan and took care of him like a kid brother, in the Reyes (of Aristocrat) fishing boat -- later Windy Imperial, Ben Sarmiento and their group, who took Juno and Rosanna with them to Batangas and elsewhere -- were the pioneers in the Philippines, dedicated divers who loved the sea, and looked upon every coral reef as a shrine and every sea wreck as a cathedral. Dempsey Pagan and Ginny Santos, daughter of Dante, even had a marriage ceremony and honeymoon underwater.

During World War II, in the San Bernardino Straits, Lingayen and Leyte Gulfs, fleets of battleships and carriers engaged in sea battles where many were sunk. There is estimated more than a million tons of cold rolled steel scrap under our seas, even after 20 percent deterioration due to oxidation, more than enough to make us a steel-making and steel-exporting nation.

There is an attempt to recover the 7,120 ton 500 foot Sigami Maru, sunk off Palomo Beach in Davao, by a C. Norton Sea Salvor Co. But its permit is stuck in the Defense Department, caught in the shuffle between Ileto and Ramos -- while $550,000 lies in a Hong Kong Bank since November, waiting to be spent in the project.

Late in the 16th century mercantilist Spain closed all foreign commerce in the Philippines except with China and Mexico. For two centuries the Manila-Acapulco galleon trade exchanged Mexican silver for the goods of China, and financed the Obras

Pias racket of the friars. Many galleons passing San Bernardino Straits and by the shores of Bicol and Batangas, were sunk by typhoons.

In Hong Kong recently Mark Hatcher sold a few pieces he excavated from an ancient Chinese trading ship sunk 150 years ago off Malaysia, which later retailed at Christie's in London for $25 million.

The 400-year old Chinese cargoes of the Manila Galleons are much more valuable. And there is one just waiting to be salvaged -- San Jose, the greatest galleon ever built, some 2,000 tons, equivalent in modern terms to carrier Enterprise -- sunk off Lubang Island near Mindoro.

For years sea salvagers concentrated in the Mediterranean and West Indies around the Bahamas. In the meantime was born the science of underwater archaeology by which sea wrecks are recovered scientifically and with due regard for valuable antique finds.

There are about 50 underwater archaeologists, 20 fully professional salvage teams, and hundreds of amateur divers in the world today, many attracted to the virgin territory of the Philippines.

Marcos PD 374 declared all sea wrecks as government property and all salvage projects involving items more than 100 years old, are entrusted to the National Museum which has little expertise on the subject.

Unfortunately, the Marcos administration and the National Museum today under Father Casal gave the salvage contract over 18,000 square miles of sea around Bicol and Batangas to an American Jew called Robert Marx. This outrageous contract gave Robert Marx monopoly over 90 percent of Manila Galleon routes, and 50 percent of the WWII wrecks, without ensuring recovery of valuable archaeological finds by the government.

This is stupid. Salvage work should be handed out ship by ship, not by wholesale grant of the entire area. A great part of our history is thus entrusted into the hands of an American treasure hunter. Dung.

Father Casal, friend of Marx, and Alfredo Evangelista (a protegé of Hans Kasten) combined to force through the contract in the face of opposition of Dr. Jesus Peralta, and in spite of the fact that there are others interested in sharing in the salvage work:

a French team under Franck Goddio, and a British team under John Rose, as well as many Filipinos with connections abroad.
March 22, 1988

Part 7. US plays poker with our lives and destinies

IT disturbs us that Chief of Staff Lisandro Abadia has gone to the USA to meet with Pentagon officials. Most likely he was given final instructions on how to deal with us brown monkeys in the 1992 elections.

It bothers us that Abadia who pathetically denied that he is an asshole, proceeded to prove that he is so by saying that the rejection of the bases treaty will only benefit the Communists. Long after McCarthyism had been discredited in the USA, assholes in our Armed Forces have been spewing the McCarthyist crap that anything that benefits the poor and the Filipinos at the expense of US militarists, US firms and the Council of Trent, must be the work of Communists.

Wholesale murders of priests and human rights workers even today show that despite the end of the Cold War, the US doctrine of Low Intensity Conflict (LIC) is still the unofficial policy of our Armed Forces.

Deborah Barry, an American expert on Low Intensity Conflict tells us that while the Chinese play a cerebral game called Go and the Russians play an intellectual game called Chess, American neanderthals play a visceral game called Poker. Poker, like the LIC, is a high stakes game, chancy and fast, where one has to use bluff and deception, not necessarily brains, and where one can get in and out fast, depending on a quick-fix solutions.

Barry reminds us that LIC is still being applied in such Third World countries as Nicaragua, El Salvador and the Philippines:

FIRST, the greatest lesson of Vietnam is that outright American intervention is counterproductive. Escalation only invites greater resistance of the nationalist forces. Therefore, the LIC seeks to use surrogate native forces, such as the AFP, vigilante groups and hired killers to do battle with the enemy, instead of risking precious American lives.

SECOND, the greatest enemy of Americans and a successful LIC campaign are Nationalism and Human Rights Advocacy. Therefore every effort must be made to equate nationalism and "secular humanism" with communism. Therefore such people as Jovy Salonga, Joker Arroyo, Rene Saguisag, Bobbit Sanchez, Sister Mariani Dimaranan, Sister Mary John Manansan, must be subjected to constant whispered accusations of being communists and deviates.

THIRD, the prime target is not territory but the population. The best way to win this war is to simplify it as a battle between the forces of good and evil, of democracy versus the evil empire of communism, a battle that must be waged at all levels, from barrio to the international level, from political to religious. This corresponds to the world-view of the Moonies who are religious lunatics, US Pentecostal Fundamentalist sects on our campuses and on TV, and such religious conservatives as the Octopus Diaboli, who think the whole world is a battlefield between God's Chosen and the forces of Satan.

FOURTH, in this high stakes LIC poker game, if victory is won the Americans gather up the winnings (bases in perpetuity, US monopolies, free trade and subsistence agriculture for the Philippines); but if defeat comes, the Americans have little to lose and the Filipinos will pay the price in terms of civil war, political paralysis, and economic catastrophe. It is for this reason, to "cover all bases,"' so to speak, that Americans ally themselves with the Council of Trent, the Octopus Diaboli, Marcos loyalists, the RAMboys and religious freaks.

FIFTH, the LIC seeks to use ``communist tactics" against the communists, retorting by reflection, blurring the distinction between military and civilian, and concentrating on the non-combatant population which it seeks to confuse, divide and neutralize. This is done by selective repression of do-gooders, such as priests (Fathers Favali, Romana, Pico, Abing, Satur), nuns, doctors (Bobby de la Paz, Dr. Escandor), labor leaders (Rolando Olalia), and newsmen. This requires a massive intelligence network, using high technology and Filipino CIA agents.

SIXTH, the LIC envisions that Americans must be able to get in and out of the conflict when American interests so dictate, but that the natives must be prepared to fight a long war of attrition, to accept internicine war as a normal way of life (with the NPA, MNLF), not so much to win but to wear down the enemies of America even to the point where both contending forces are both forced to the point of collapse. The interest of America, not that of her friends, is paramount.

SEVENTH, to make America again Number One, to shatter the Vietnam syndrome, the LIC postulates that everything that happens in the world is a battle between the forces of good and evil; that no accommodation or compromise is ever possible between democratic forces (which includes Marcos and the Shah) and the communists (which include priests and nuns who care for the poor); that what benefits one side must necessarily be a disadvantage to the other.

Americans play poker with our lives and destinies.
December 1991, Philippine Daily Inquirer

Part 8. Drugs here 14 times dearer than abroad

The Americans, I believe, would rather kill all Filipinos than allow the amendment of our patent laws. During Martial Law, the UP Law Center (UPLC) made a historic proposal to do just that, but the American Chamber and the Embassy were able to strong-arm and bribe Marcos Technocrats to further strengthen American monopoly by getting Marcos to sign a decree to "protect intellectual property" without any reciprocal concessions to the Philippines.

The UPLC asks: If we have no patents for Americans to protect, why should we protect theirs?

The UPLC wanted to amend our patent laws to exclude protection on products and product applications, in line with the patent laws of most other nations.

Most nations grant patents only on the PROCESS, not the PRODUCT; and take steps to ensure that protection is not extended unless the process is actually used in the country in order to generate employment and disseminate the know-how.

The Philippines is one of two countries that is unique in the sense that it protects the patent holder not only from the unauthorized use of the process, but also from the sale of competitive products.

Thus by getting a Philippine Patent, the foreign drug company gets a Monopoly on the entire Philippine market, simply by preventing the unauthorized importation of competitive products from other sources, and/or preventing anyone else from manufacturing it in the Philippines.

Thus some broad-spectrum antibiotics are sold in the Philippines at 20 times the price they are sold in Europe, where the patent laws are different. Many countries protect themselves from the abuses of multinational drug companies without denying themselves access to new drugs.

Countries that do not provide Product Patents for medicinal and pharmaceutical drugs are Argentina, Brazil, Canada, Chile, Columbia, Denmark, Ecuador, Egypt, Greece, Iceland, Iran, Israel, South Korea, Luxembourg, Morocco, New Zealand, Norway, Peru, Portugal, Italy, and Switzerland (which happens to be the largest exporter of pharmaceutical products). Brazil and South Korea do not even grant Process Patents on pharmaceutical products.

Despite the representations of the bright boys of the UP Law Center, foreigners were able to get our Marcos Technocrats to further amend our patent law to give Multinational corporations even greater opportunity for abuse under "protection of intellectual property".... which gives foreigners a patent monopoly on our drugs as well as copyright monopolies on old old movies on Betamax.

How sad!

The American multinationals in the drug industry own 90 percent of all the patents issued in this country, and therefore have a secure monopoly position in the Philippines. The Philippines thus protects the interest of Americans at the expense of the health and well-being of its own people.

Out of 16 drug manufacturers, 13 are multinationals with 57 percent of the market; and out of the 12 major drug importers, 10 are multinationals with 60 percent of the market.

The UP Law Center studies of 1978 show how American drug companies abuse the Filipino people: Ampicillin sells 4.10 times higher here than in Malaysia; Tetracyline, 7.24 times; Chloramphenicol, 3.84 times; Erythromycin, 5.44 times. Librium sells here 8.67 times more than in Great Britain, and Valium an incredible 14.29 times.

Transfer pricing abuse is rampant among foreign drug companies. Ampicillin was imported by Bristol/Mead Johnson at $242.99/kg while Doctors Pharmaceutical imported the same at $81.38/kg, a factor of 3 times. Tetracycline was imported by Bristol at $130.51/kg while the same was imported by United Lab at

$18.80/kg, a factor of 7 times! What bloodsuckers American drug companies are!

Why do we allow these things to happen? Why do we accept this situation as if it were the most natural thing in the world? Why should we risk our lives fighting Communists and Secessionists to preserve a nation that gives us no hope for a better life, a nation that reserves for the Americans the wealth and patrimony which should properly belong to its own citizens?

When this country has no more to offer, Americans can leave for the USA laden with the riches of the white man's burden, while we Filipinos are left to pay the price of poverty, ignorance and injustice with our freedom and very lives.

Dung.
June 2, 1988

Part 9. Taiwan Air Agreement and American AWAC surveillance

You know me, I do not like Americans who interfere with the Philippines' development as a nation, especially those Neanderthals in the Embassy, State Department and the American Central Intelligence Agency who dictate to us our foreign and economic policy, and destabilize our government to advance their own interest. And it would distress us no end if they promote a military take-over, damn them.

But it distresses them even more that we frustrate their designs to extradite Mark Jimenez for mail fraud, illegal political contributions and money laundering. Somehow the US Drug Enforcement Agency (DEA) got the idea into its pinhead that Erap's Financial Genius friend is involved in money laundering for the drug syndicate in Miami, and may be easily pressured into giving evidence to convict drug lords – which is of the highest priority in that poor drug addicted land. There's nothing, absolutely nothing, the USA would not do to solve its drug problem, even go to war and kidnap leaders of other countries, as it did with Panama's President Manuel Noriega. It must distress Americans no end to see Mark Jimenez waxing in the lap of luxury in Forbes Park, with the fruits of his brokering the PLDT and PCIB deals, dreaming of brokering a Meralco deal, protected by security forces and our Supreme Court.

Again it distresses the Americans that our Air Agreement with Taiwan was effectively cancelled by our Air Agreement with mainland China. Our Air Agreement with Taiwan allows EVA Airline of Taipei to discharge and pick up passengers in Manila and bring them to the USA directly (against treaty provisions) for a measly US $780 per round-trip, while PAL charges US $ 1,400 for the same trip. The world-class accommodations of EVA Airlines include an in-between class between Business and Economy that allows passengers to have a much wider seat and many of the privileges of the Business Class. PAL simply cannot compete. And so it became imperative to cancel the Taiwan Air Agreement to allow our national airline to make some money on the Philippine-USA run. On the other hand, our Air Agreement with China gives PAL a lucrative route ferrying passengers from Manila to and from Xiamen, Shanghai and Beijing. There is no doubt about it, business-wise, the interest of the Philippines is better served doing business with China rather than Taiwan. We cannot have both under our One-China Policy.

This distresses the Neanderthal Americans no end, because our Taiwan Air Agreement is part of their secret defense strategy. The Americans have been behind many bilateral Air Agreements in our part of the world, which ordinarily is none of their fucking business. But above many commercial flights of other countries, flying at 30,000 feet, flies an American surveillance plane called the E-3B Sentry AWAC, flying at 60,000 feet and doing spy work for the American Defense Department. This plane has a dome-shaped radar contrivance that can scan a wide area below, unobserved because the commercial plane underneath shields it from the radar of America's enemies below. It has been said inside intelligence circles that the Korean commercial plane shot down when it crossed into the Russian airspace, was destroyed because the AWAC spy plane above swerved a bit to the side, exposing its position to the computer-aimed heat-seeking missiles of the Russians below, and triggering an automatic response. When the AWAC plane swerved back to above the Korean plane, the Russian missile changed direction and slammed into the poor commercial plane. While Koreans and the world condemned this act of "treachery," the American CIA and Defense Department maintained a tight-lipped silence.

This is the kind of game that our cancellation of the Taiwan Air Agreement has prevented the US military from playing in the South China Sea, and this is one reason the Americans are really pissed off with us. The E-3B Sentry AWAC has for its primary function, airborne surveillance and command control communications. It has a speed slow enough and a size small enough to hide behind a commercial plane below: airspeed of 360 miles per hour, wing span of 130 feet 10 inches; length 145 feet 6 inches; height 41 feet 4 inches; radar dome 30 feet diameter, 6 feet thick, mounted 11 feet above the fuselage; range, more than 8 hours without refueling; with a crew of 17 to 23 persons.
January 31, 2000

ooooo

Chapter Six:
DR. ALAN BEER'S BABIES

Part 1. Hope for women with recurrent miscarriages

Many women who have had recurrent miscarriages are told time and again by their doctors that it is God's will and that they should try again. Oftentimes, trying again causes even more heartbreak. After several miscarriages, her doctors tell her that "It was not meant to be" or "There was nothing you can do about it, it is God's will."

More often than not, it is not the reproduction system that is the problem. The problem may be the immune system rejecting the fetus as a foreign object, according to Dr. Alan Beer, pioneer in Reproductive Immunology, who is scheduled to address the annual meeting of Philippine Obstetrics and Gynecology Society on November 15 and 16, and will also deliver a lecture to the general public, especially women with miscarriage problems, earlier on Sunday, November 12 from 9 to 11 AM, at the Westin Plaza Hotel in the CCP Complex, Roxas Boulevard. Those interested may register at the Secretariat of the Reproductive Immunology Center, at the Suite 1601 Medical Plaza, on Amorsolo Street corner de la Rosa behind Makati Medical Center. Call Ms. Helen Yap, telephone 752-5254 for details.

Dr. Alan Beer, a professor of Microbiology and Immunology, as well as Obstetrics and Gynecology, Director of Reproductive Medicine at Finch University of Health Sciences and the Chicago Medical School, has done 25 years of research in infertility and immunology by studying couples who achieve a pregnancy only to lose it repeatedly to miscarriage. This can happen even when healthy embryos are produced and transplanted in the uterus via *in vitro* fertilization, but still fail to implant in the uterus and thus, do not result in a full-term pregnancy.

According to Dr. Alan Beer, the problem lies mainly in the immune system where embryos are misinterpreted by the immune system as foreign bodies or even cancer cells, and thereby reject it. What Dr. Alan Beer, pioneer in this new field in both Finch University of Health Sciences and in the Chicago Medical School, has discovered in his 25 years of pioneering research on recurrent miscarriages, is that we can do something about it. Dr. Beer has committed his professional life to studying the causes of infertility in couples who have experienced multiple miscarriages. He has discovered that the immune systemis most often to blame, since in the case of some women, it attacks the fetus the way it would cancer cells. The more miscarriages you experience, the stronger and quicker it attacks in subsequent pregnancies. In some cases, it happens after the birth of the first child.

There have been many studies authored by Dr. Beer on how to down-regulate the immune system in order to allow it to accept your fetus. Dr. Beer will also inaugurate Reproductive Immunology Center in Medical Plaza on November 11. This Center is one out only ten such centers in the world, the first and only one in Southeast Asia, under Dr. Eduardo Lim, MD (UERM '83), the only Reproductive Immunologist in the Philippines and Southeast Asia.

My daughter, Rosanna Henares Angeles has this kind of problem. In six years of married life with Eric Angeles, she experienced 5 miscarriages, one at 13 weeks of pregnancy and the next two at 7 weeks; and another 2 "chemical miscarriages" wherein the pregnancy test showed a positive reading, only to be disappointed by a negative reading and bleeding after a few weeks. She will tell her story in this space tomorrow.

Part 2. In 6 years, Rosanna had 5 miscarriages
I give the floor to my daughter Rosanna Henares Angeles for her urgent message to women with pregnancy problems:

When my brother Ronnie sired his first child, I was 14 years old. Then when I held Celine in my arms, I knew that one day, I just had to be a mother. I never knew that such a simple wish would be such a difficult endeavor. In our six years of married life, my husband Eric and I have experienced 5 miscarriages, one at 13 weeks of pregnancy and the next two at 7 weeks pregnancy, and also 2 chemical miscarriages wherein the pregnancy test showed a positive reading, only to be disappointed by a negative reading and bleeding after a few weeks.

When I asked my first Obstetrician-Gynecologist what had happened, her only explanation was that it was a freak accident and that it was not meant to be. Three doctors and countless number of excuses after, I finally met Dr. Eduardo Lim, MD, who specialized in Internal Medicine, then specialized further in "Allergy and Immunology," then sub-specialized in "Reproductive Immunology" at the UCLA. These smorgasbord of specialties opened a new hope for me and for many women who have a history of multiple miscarriages.

After taking a battery of tests , Dr. Eduardo Lim (no relation to the stockbroker) finally introduced us to the enemy "The Immune System."

The Immune System is a wonderful network of cells and molecules like antibodies that are there to fight disease. The reason an AIDS (Acquired Immune Deficiency Syndrome) patient dies is because his immune system has lost its ability to fight diseases, so he dies of pneumonia, diabetes, TB, cancer, or whatever else.

My immune system is the exact opposite. It is vigilant, it is strong, it is hardworking… but, sadly it is also not very bright. My immune system fails to recognize the fetus and misinterprets it as a foreign object, much like what happens when it encounters cancer cells. It therefore attacks the fetus instead of nurturing it, thereby causing a miscarriage. Studies by the pioneer Dr. Alan Beer of the Chicago Medical School/ Finch University of Health Science have shown that the more miscarriages you have experienced, the faster the immune system detects the "enemy". The uterus then behaves like a den of lions leaving little hope that the fetus will survive.

Part 3. The immunity problem that causes miscarriages

Rosanna continues:

Dr. Alan Beer has done extensive research on infertility by studying couples who get pregnant easily then lose every pregnancy through miscarriage.

There are five categories of immune problems that can cause pregnancy loss, In Vitro Fertilization (IVF) failures and infertility. You can be afflicted with only one category, or in the more difficult cases, 4 or 5 of the categories. They are very confusing to the untrained non-medical mind and it took a while for me to understand them.

CATEGORY 1. This is when you and your husband have a similar genetic makeup. This is perfect if you were to donate a kidney to your spouse, but for reproduction, it results in a lack of blocking anti-bodies. In simple English it means that the normal reaction is to first recognize the fetus. This recognition signals the immune system to produce BLOCKING ANTIBODIES which prevent rejecting from attacking the placenta. It also serves as fertilizer for placental growth and maturation. Since you and your husband are alike, the normal process of recognition is weak, so no blocking antibodies are manufactured. This leaves the rejecting anti-bodies to wreak havoc on the placenta.

CATEGORY 2. This is the most common category. It is called APAS or Anti-Phospholipid Antibody Syndrome. Phospholipids are the glue molecules for implantation and placentation. What happens is that your blood is too thick, making you prone to blood clots. In my case, a blood clot formed in my uterus and it was obstructing the flow of blood (which carries needed nutrients) from reaching the fetus.

CATEGORY 3. This is similar to APAS except that the antibodies developed are particularly against the baby's DNA or DNA breakdown products, as reflected by a positive Anti-Nuclear Antibody test.

CATEGORY 4. This is when you have anti-sperm antibodies, meaning your body mucus doesn't react well to sperm and therefore renders them immobile. Even if your husband has a healthy sperm count, your mucus traps the sperm and doesn't allow them the freedom to get to your egg.

CATEGORY 5. This is when you have elevated Natural Killer Cells and as the name suggests, your body is vigilant against all foreign objects including the fetus. You can imagine vigilante marines in your uterus killing everything in sight. These Natural Killer Cells also known as Vigilante Marines think that they are protecting you by killing an innocent bystander, your fetus.

Dr. Ed Lim's patients are mostly in their 30's, partly because the trend is now to marry late. Furthermore, most patients see their regular OB-Gynecologists and are only referred to Dr. Ed Lim (a Reproductive Immunologist) after 3 miscarriages.

Most of us are often without hope, perplexed by a problem we do not know, and often face misinformed OB-Gynecologists telling us to try again, it was not meant to be, the body knows when a baby is weak and needs to be rejected, and other excuses that don't get you in touch with the real problem.

With each advice, our immune systems get stronger and our dreams go further and further away.

Part 4. Coming here is Pioneer Dr. Alan Beer, Reproductive Immunologist
Rosanna continues:
Those of you who are interested to know more about Immune Problems Causing Infertility, may be fortunate to know that the first pioneer and ultimate authority on this subject, Dr. Alan Beer from the Chicago Medical School and Finch University of Health Sciences, will come to the Philippines to give a lecture to the general public (especially husbands with wives having miscarriage problems) at the Westin Philippine Plaza Hotel, CCP Complex, Roxas Boulevard, on Sunday November 12, from 9 AM to 11 AM. Registration fee is P1,000 per couple to cover venue and snacks. Interested parties should register at the Reproductive Immunology Center, Suite 1601 Medical Plaza, Amorsolo corner de la Rosa, right behind Makati Medical Center. Call Miss Helen Yap of the Secretariat at telephone 752-5254 for details.

Dr. Alan Beer will also inaugurate the new Reproductive Immunology Center under Dr. Eduardo Lim at the Medical Plaza, on November 11. The Center will be one of the ten such centers in the world, the first and only one in Southeast Asia. There are five in the USA, and one each in Greece, South America, Japan, and Columbia.

Dr. Alan Beer will also address the annual meeting of the Philippine Obstetrics and Gynecology Society, with a technical lecture for doctors on November 15 and 16, 2000, also at the Westin Philippine Plaza.

Dr. Alan Beer of the Chicago Medical School/ Finch University of Health Sciences, pioneer in Productive Immunology will be coming to the Philippines to deliver a series of lectures on his discovery that certain infertility problems are caused not by the reproductive system as we initially assume, but by the immune system. The immune system's main objective is to protect our body by fighting infections and tumors. When each fight has been won, it should shut down. Not so with certain women.

Dr. Alan Beer and his team have identified a relatively new auto-immune disorder called Antiphospholipid Antibody Syndrome or APAS, and this discovery has given hundreds of women who thought they were infertile new-found hope of having a baby. APAS is usually not diagnosed until a woman has had three miscarriages. In half of the cases, she has already borne a first child.

APAS is an auto-immune disorder which is caused by the presence of the lupus anticoagulant, although having it may not necessarily mean you have the lupus disease. In simple terms, APAS causes the body to produce antibodies that adhere to the walls of the blood vessels. If left undetected and untreated, APAS can cause blood clots and even strokes. When a woman achieves a pregnancy, APAS can cause the clotting of the vessels in the placenta, blocking life-giving nutrients to the growing fetus. Most women with APAS have no apparent symptoms and the disorder is only revealed by a blood test called KCT (Keratin Clotting Time.)

Since the blood is thick or in hyper-coagulable condition, treatment for APAS involves keeping the blood thin, so if a blood clot occurs in the blood vessels, particularly in the uterus, hopefully it is not significant enough to cause a problem.

Thinning the blood can be done in a number of ways, depending on your KCT test or the levels of antibodies present. Some women only need to take a daily dose of baby aspirin (Aspilets 80 mg.) during their pregnancy, while others must inject themselves with one to two shots of the blood thinner called heparin (Clexan, Lovenox). This discovery is amazing news for women who may have thought that they were unable to carry a child to term. A simple blood test may now detect why a woman has miscarried in the past, and offer new hope for the future.

Part 5. The heart-breaking story of Riana and her child
Rosanna continues:
Seven years ago, Riana Trajano was in Canada, pregnant with Mon Trajano's and her first child. The pregnancy went on smoothly with absolutely no hitches. After a few years, the couple wanted to have another child and thought the process would be as simple as the first. For months they had gone to their OB/Gyn to track her ovulation cycle, taking Clomid for 4 cycles in order to produce eggs. Every month was an emotional ride as they waited for good news of a positive pregnancy. None came.

When they felt the stress was overbearing, they stopped the work up. Happily, she showed up at her obstetrician's clinic

12 weeks into her second pregnancy. The problem with APAS is that blood clots position themselves in different parts of the body including the uterus, and their presence obstruct the flow of nutrients to the fetus. With Riana, they detected numerous blood clots and at 20 weeks the baby, starved of needed nutrition, was only as big as a 17-week old. It was a bad start and she had been warned that it is better for an APAS victim to detect a pregnancy within 4 weeks.

Still, Riana wanted this baby and did whatever was medically possible to keep that child. Dr. Eduardo Lim, her Reproductive Immunologist, tried to make up for lost time. Her blood clots had worsened making it imperative for her to stay in the hospital for 4 months. Despite all this, she delivered her baby prematurely at 28 weeks, with the baby weighing only 1 ½ pounds. They named him Michael, and he was brought to the infant ICU where he made a brave attempt to fight for his life. Every day, Riana sang to him, caressed him, loved him. Everyday, his brother Christopher visited him and encouraged him to live so he could have a brother, and he promised to take care of him. After 3 months which felt like a lifetime, Michael decided to die, leaving his family, Mon, Riana and Christopher heartbroken. It was such a traumatic experience that Mon and Riana couldn't think of having another child and of having to undergo the same ordeal. But with Michael watching over them and giving them hope, Riana had found herself pregnant a third time. This time, APAS was detected earlier and although she gave birth to a 8 month premature baby weighing 3 pounds 5 ounces, Anthony, who was armed with a good set of lungs and with an almost 100 percent chance of surviving.

Anthony is now turning 1 year old. His older brother Christopher loves him and is thankful for having a brother. But Michael is still very much part of the family. Mon and Riana are certain that he watches over them every night, their own valiant angel, making sure that his brothers are safe and his earthly family whole.

Part 6. Elena, another patient
Rosanna concludes:
Another patient Elena experienced 12 years of infertility and was a graduate of all the infertility treatments available this

side of the earth. She had to endure having to go to reunions and parties with all her relatives asking the inevitable "Wala pa ba? Bakit?" She had undergone 6 or more artificial inseminations and had one ectopic pregnancy, one blighted pregnancy, and one early miscarriage. Just when all hope was gone, she consulted Dr. Ed Lim, the only Reproductive Immunologist in Southeast Asia. Elena and her husband were found to be genetically similar, a situation seemingly harmless but actually confuses our immune system and sends it off-balance. In Reproductive Immunology, this syndrome is known as Absence of Blocking Anti Bodies.

Dr. Ed Lim gave her Lymphocyte Immune Therapy (LIT) wherein she had to get 6 friends of the same blood type to donate a bag of blood each. Their blood was then processed and injected into her subcutaneously. The purpose of LIT is to remind the immune system that to keep a pregnancy, it has to achieve two steps. Step 1 is to recognize a foreign presence in the body and reject it momentarily. This initial rejection brings about Step 2 wherein the Blocking Antibodies move in to protect the fetus and nurture it. In other words, it is important for the initial threat to appear so the good guys (Blocking Antibodies) appear. You can compare these Blocking Antibodies to soldiers who wield truncheons and shields to prevent the unruly mob (rejecting Anti Bodies) from overpowering and destroying the placenta.

After her treatment, Elena became pregnant. She gave birth to a healthy 7-pound baby girl named Elisha who is now 3 years old, and very recently became an Ate to Gabriel Carl who was born recently on October 21, 2000, 15 years after Elena and Carlos first dreamed of having a child..

Thank God for Dr. Alan Beer and Dr. Eduardo Lim. Meet them when they lecture in Westin Plaza Hotel Sunday, November 12 from 9 to 11 AM. Damage: P1,000 per couple to cover venue and snacks.

November 6-10, 2000 for the Philippine Post

ooooo

Chapter Seven:
SHADOWS ON THE WALL

Part 1. BATTLE OF THE SEXES

Prelude: The Creation of Man and Woman
Fade in the Credits: God Almighty (Ronnie Henares); Adam (Danby Henares); Eve (Susan Reyes) – all actors about 15 to 21 years of age

NARRATOR: *We give you God Almighty creating Man and Woman!*

God Almighty takes a bow and proceeds with His pantomime.

He forms a man out of a pile of clay (invisible to the audience); forms the head and the chest, pounds on the chest; then the legs; ponders on the Man; decides to give him a male organ, which he carefully shapes and attaches. He clicks his fingers, and Voila, Adam appears, and faces the audience.

Now he forms the Woman, her Coca-Cola shape; her head and her hair; he shapes a ball of clay into a breast and attaches it, it falls, he picks it up and re-installs it; he shapes another ball of clay into a breast, attaches it, and shapes the teats; then he looks around to see if anyone is watching; turns his back furtively and with his fingers at the back, he shapes the clit. He clicks his fingers, and voila, Eve appears, and turns around.

Adam and Eve look at each other, and start quarrelling; God Almighty intervenes, and makes them understand that they should make love and make a baby. He gets Adam to carry Eve into the bedroom, shuts the door, and congratulates himself.

God Almighty suddenly realizes that there is bedlam in the bedroom, pounds on the door; the door opens, Adam staggers out, he is dragged back in and the door slams shut; God pounds on the door, in vain, and he panics at what is happening inside; finally he stops, gives up and shrugs his shoulders.

Bell rings as the Titles fade in: BATTLES OF THE SEXES in 3 ROUNDS…

Round One: The Secret Life of Mr. Castro, based on James Thurber's Secret Life of Walter Mitty, starring Elvira

Henares (wife) and Tommy de Castro (husband), both about 16 years of age.

Silent film with musical background. Starts with scene of car, driven by Tommy with nagging wife Elvira (mournful music).

Tommy falls into a reverie that he is driving a race car in a Grand Prix event (lively music). Protracted race. He wins the cup surrounded by fans and an adoring wife Elvira.

Tommy reverts back to reality, driving his jalopy beside a nagging wife. He almost hits a pedestrian and stops. Tommy and Elvira get down to placate the pedestrian who is unharmed and fuming with indignation. Elvira shoves him aside, and continues to nag her husband Tommy. The irate pedestrian separates them, and knocks Tommy unconscious.

Tommy now dreams that he is being lulled to sleep by three beautiful slave girls. Elvira appears, signals the slave girls to go away and lovingly cradles her husband in her arms.

Tommy, back to reality, is awakened by Elvira. They get back to the car and drive home. Elvira still nagging. They approach the front door, Elvira angrily pushes him away, enters the house and slams the door shut.

His back to the wall, Tommy lights up a cigarette (music Nelson Eddy singing Stouthearted Men) and imagines he is being blindfolded, facing a Firing Squad. They fire and Tommy slumps to the ground, the wall behind him smeared with blood. Like Jose Rizal, Tommy dies a hero's death. THE END.

Round Two: Camison Ni Rosa, starring Rosanna Henares (Rosa), Daniel Dioquino (husband), Minnie Dioquino (mother-in-law), Cindy Dioquino (wife), Ninoy Dioquino (boyfriend of Rosa) – all actors, grossly miscast. From 6 to 12 years of age.

Silent film, with musical background. It starts with the Dioquino Family having breakfast. The Mother-in-law is nagging the Husband who in a moment of disgust attacked his fried eggs with a knife. Mother-in-law continuous to nag, signals the Wife to go out with her to shop. Wife kisses Husband and leaves with her mother, leaving Husband alone in the house.

Scene shifts a hand knocking at the door, zooms out to show Rosa, holding a case of clothes. The door is opened by the husband. Rosa explains that her car stalled and asks to use the phone. Husband welcomes her in.

Rosa uses the phone, while the Husband flirts with her, and seduces her with a bottle of whisky. Rosa puts down the phone, and both began a party of two, drinking and fornicating.

Scene shifts to a hand knocking at the door, zooms out to show Mother-in-law, with Wife in tow.

Inside the house, the Rosa and husband sober up and Rosa prepared to leave, lifting her case of clothes which opens and spills its contents to the floor. She scoops them up into her case, inadvertently leaving behind her camison (under-dress worn instead of a brassiere) under the table.

Husband opens the door, to welcome his nagging Mother-in-law and wife, with Rosa hiding behind the door sneaks out unnoticed. The door shuts, with Mother-in-law still nagging.

Mother-in-law sees Rosa's camison under the table. What the hell is this? she screamed. Husband explains that he bought it for his favorite Mother-in-law, and she is pleased.

Scene shifts to later that night, with the Dioquino family having a party. Frenzied dancing by guests.

Knock on the front door which is opened by the Husband. Rosa and her boyfriend Ninoy at the threshold, demanding the return of the missing camison. Ninoy grabs Husband by the throat and threatens him. Husband assents and closes the door.

A finger closes the light at the party room, and in the blackness, we hear screams and pandemonium. The light is turned on and the Mother-in-law hides behind an upturned table, absolutely naked, her dress on the floor, cursing to high heavens.

The front door opens, and the missing camiso is handed to Rosa and her boyfriend. Husband closes the door and fall to the floor fainting with relief. THE END.

Round Three: The Last Supper, starring Atom Henares and Kelly Periquet…

Atom in the living room, stares at Kelly's painting. He thinks:

ATOM: Well, Kelly, my darling, tonight is the night, our last fling, the bash to end all bashes. The end, literally, because tomorrow, we are back to the poor house, the end to all elegant living, the end to all our dreams and great expectations. It is hard to believe that we have lost everything – the business, the house, the jewels, everything. I cannot see how I can start again, impossible, I am too old. My credit standing all gone, my business reputation shattered, what else is left to me? Unless, unless… it is a good thing my wife and I insured each other for one million pesos each when we got married….

Kelly in the bedroom, applying her make-up. She thinks:

KELLY: I must be beautiful tonight, I must! Poor Atom, all these years life has been good to us – a successful business, a beautiful house, trips around the world, wonderful parties, expensive jewels, everything – now all gone, nothing left except a million pesos in insurance, but we can't even have that unless we are dead. Poor Atom! I must be beautiful tonight.

Back to Atom, he thinks:

ATOM: Oh my darling Kelly, if I die, you can have all our riches back, the beautiful house, the jewelries, your expensive parties, everything we lost! If you die… what am I saying??

They meet in the dining room.

ATOM: Kelly, my princess, how beautiful you are tonight! Tonight is your night. Anything you want – the sun, the moon, the stars…

KELLY: I want only you, my darling, only you!

ATOM *(offering her a chair)*: May I, your highness? Oh yes, the champagne…

Atom thinks:

ATOM: How beautiful she looks tonight! Poor Kelly, poor spoiled Kelly, she never knew what it is to be poor. I cannot stand the thought of her skimping on expenses, doing without the latest fashions, cleaning house, washing dishes…. better dead than to live like that. Dead… *(he puts poison into his own glass of champagne)*

KELLY: Oh my darling Atom, I know how much you must be suffering. You gave me everything, and now you have nothing…

Atom thinks:

ATOM: A million pesos! What I can do with a million pesos – I can start all over again, recoup my losses, save the business!

Kelly thinks:

KELLY: Oh no, I know that look of Atom. I saw it once before, when he makes a terrible decision. Oh no, it can't be! He is thinking of…. he is thinking of killing himself!

ATOM: My darling Kelly, I cannot imagine how you can survive being poor. And I'll do something about it. I promise, my darling, I promise. *(he switches their glasses)*
Kelly thinks:
KELLY: Oh God, I cannot let him kill himself. He gave me everything, all he had. He deserves better. I'd rather kill myself. I can do no less for him. Oh Atom, let me die so you can live! *(kisses him)* Now, I shall switch glasses *(switches glasses)*, and take his poisoned glass… *(they raise their glasses)* To us forever, for richer or poorer…
ATOM: For better or for worse….
KELLY: In sickness or in health…
BOTH: Till death do us part…..
They drink, the door closes as Atom falls to the floor. Fade out as Kelly screams:
KELLY: Atom! Atom! Oh my God!!

The Decision: *Bell rings, title flashes The Battle of the Sexes, The weaker sex WINS by technical knock-out. THE ULTIMATE END.*

PART 2. RAIN, based on a story by Somerset Maugham, starring Sylvia Lichauco and Joviboy Cruz, at the ages of 12.
Scene: a rainstorm called siam-siam *which lasts for 18 days.*
Scene: A prostitute enjoying her profession, making good money and having fun with her friends and customers.
Scene: A priest who apparently cannot stand others having fun.
The priest resents the party in the above apartment, comes up, invades the premises, and denounced the prostitute as a slut, and her friends as pimps and profligates.
The prostitute tries to make friends with the priest, but he slaps her down, and yells that he will have her branded by the police as a woman of ill repute.
Rain, rain, it just won't stop raining.
The next day the prostitute is called to the police station, where she was questioned and warned to behave. She pleads for mercy, and is told to go to hell.

Rain continues to pour. Tradition dictates that if the rain lasts nine days, it will continue for another nine days. That is why this storm is called siam-siam.

That night the prostitute knocks at the priest's door, and consumed with guilt for whatever crime she is accused of, she kneels and begs for his forgiveness. He hands her the Good Book and tells her to pray with him and sin no more.

The pouring rain lulled the prostitute to sleep. The priest endures the kind of hell every man endures when in the presence of a desirable woman. My God, even a priest, even a holy man. He touches her.

Rain, rain, it never stopped raining. It was a stormy night for both, sharing a nightmare of unbelievable guilt.

The prostitute wakes hours later and realizes what has happened. Pigs! she screams, all you men are pigs! And throws the crucifix at the priest.

He leaves, followed by all his demons, exploding with the lightning, and the thunder and the rain, and black as hell from pole to pole, and is seen dead, a suicide, on the ground with his crucifix.

The prostitute's room is heaven is full of joy, and lust and music.

The rain keeps pouring out its tears, and vomit. The music rises to a climax. The End.

PART 3. THE MONKEY'S PAW, based on a story by W. W. Jacobs, starring Sylvia Lichauco (wife), Joviboy Cruz (man); Ronnie Henares (son); Atom Henares (driver)…the cast from 5 to 12 years f age.

NARRATOR: A very holy man wanted to prove that FATE ruled men's lives, and that anyone who interfered with FATE, did so to his own sorrow._He cast a spell on a mummified monkey's paw so that anyone can have Three Wishes on it. This monkey's paw found its way into the possession of one man, his wife and their son. This is their tragic story.

MAN: This magical monkey's paw given to me by a friend will grant three wishes to any man. Three wishes! Any wishes you would like to have? Any wish at all? On this lovely peaceful night, I will grant any wish you want.

WIFE: Oh, I do not know. We already have everything there is to wish for – food on the table, a roof over our head, clothes on our back, a loving marriage and a wonderful son -- and all the amenities of a civilized and happy life.

SON: Well, there is something I would like to have – money. Look at my wallet, empty. What I want is lots of money to buy me an expensive first class hi-fidelity sound system to while my peaceful hours away. How about it, papa? Wish me a lot of money!

MAN: That is an excellent idea, son. Our first wish, oh god of fate, is for lots of money. Oops! It moved, oh my god, it moved! Did you see that?

SON: Oh papa, I did not see it move. You are just imagining things. Magical monkey's paw, my athlete's foot, it's a fraud! Three wishes! It is just wishful thinking. Oh well, papa, mama, I have to go, I have a meeting with a friend. Bye, see you later, alligator. Do not forget, if the money comes, it belongs to my wallet.

NARRATOR: At this point of our story, we introduce you to Alfredo Tomas, whom we call Atom – A for Alfredo, Tom for Tomas, Atom Bum, B-U-M. But he is no bum, he is the millionaire we wrote about in our other movie, Atom the Great. Atom the Great, the rich spoiled brat has just bought a new Rolls-Royce car which he is now testing on the road to determine its maximum speed - 50, 60, 70, 80, 90, 100 miles per hour, and still running even faster. Wow!

NARRATOR: On the same street not far away ....
Son walks.

ATOM: Faster! Faster! Faster! Whatta car! I bet I can make this car go even faster!
Son walks.

ATOM: 120, 130, 150, 160. Wow! It's a train, it's a plane, it's Superman!
Son walks.

ATOM: Wow! I am the King of the World!

SON: (gets hit) My God! Oooooooh!!

The accident victim is carried off. The scene shifts to the morgue. Atom is seen signing a check and hands it over to the Father who stares blankly at the check.

WIFE: (crying) What happened to my son? My son! (uncovers the sheet, screams)

The scene shifts to the bedroom.

WIFE: (crying) Oh my poor son, my son! We have more wishes! Make the second wish. Wish my son back alive! I want my son back alive!

MAN: Oh no! He is dead, mutilated, dead three days ago, he is nothing but broken bones and rotting flesh! *(the Monkey's Paw moves!)* No! No! He is dead, broken and rotting, we can't have him back! This is horrible! Horrible!

WIFE (scrambling to the door): My son! My son is back!

Man: The third wish, the last wish! Where is the monkey's paw? Where is it?

The boy pounding on the door. The wife, fumbling with the door knob.

WIFE: How do I open this door? Help. I want my son back!

MAN: I wish… I wish… !
The Monkey's Paw moves.
MAN: I wish he is dead!
The door opens. Wife screams. Camera scans through empty space, music rises.
WIFE: (inaudibly) My son, my son.
The music rises to a climax. The End.

PART 4. JUDY GARLAND AND LIZA MINELLI

We have often heard from our parents of a great movie called *Wizard Of Oz* which won the Academy Award, of a great song that won the first Oscar for the Best Song of the Year, *Somewhere Over The Rainbow*, and a great superstar who starred in the picture and sang the song, Judy Garland. We also know that Judy Garland was the mother of one of the greatest singers we have today, Liza Minelli.

What few of us know is that when Judy Garland starred in the *Wizard of Oz* at the tender age of 12, she was given barbiturates to keep up her energy level, and became all her life a drug addict. She was unhappily married three times and ended up taking her own life, a suicide. Judy's drug addiction, her divorces, and her suicide caused many scars in the emotional make-up of her daughter, Liza Minelli, a lonely child who thought she was ugly and unloved. Yet she tries to remember the few happy times she had with her mother, knowing that her mother Judy Garland was a great artist who shed so many tears to bring to all of us so much pleasure, so much joy. Liza remembers her mother, just out of the mental asylum, making her last public appearance among many adoring fans, singing for the last time:

Somewhere over the rainbow, way up high / There's a land that I've heard of / Once in a lullaby / Someday I'll wish upon a star / And wake up where the clouds are far behind me / Where troubles melt like lemon drops / Way above the chimney tops / That's where you'll find me / Somewhere over the rainbow, bluebirds fly / Birds fly over the rainbow, why, oh why can't I?

Years later, Liza Minelli remembered this poignant occasion, and the few happy times she had with her unhappy mother, and sang in one of her TV specials, smiling through her tears for the one great star who shed so many tears to give all the rest of us so much sunshine, smiles and laughter, this sad and happy song:

It was a good time, it was the best time / It was a party just to be near you / It was a good time, it was the best time / And we believed that it would last forever / We would spend together, and share together / This never ever, or morning after / It was a good time, it was the best time / It seemed a short time, but such a good time / Since you've gone and won't be mine again / There are many stars that will not shine again / Except sometimes between my memories / You'd return and then, I'd remember when / It was a good time, it was the best time / It was a party just to be near you / It was a good time.

1986

ooooo

Chapter Eight: THE PHILIPPINES

Part 1. The Love Affairs Of Teresita Valdez

Teresita Valdez is an ordinary housewife married to a policeman who once got into an accident, suffered seven broken ribs and a fractured left arm, was paralyzed for 8 months and 11 days, and was never the same again. At the time Teresita was working as a dressmaker in my wife's factory, Henlich Mark which made wooden toys and children's costumes.

Teresita Valdez in time became the production manager of the factory, had an only child named Arturo Jr., was for some time the chief breadwinner of the family, and was faithfully associated with my wife for almost 30 years. Little did we know till only recently that Tessie, now production coordinator of Daiichi Densi Electronics, was involved in several love affairs, eight of them at last count. And she spent the money too as a sort of Sugar Mammy. Why, oh why did you do it, Tessie? "Oh, I did it for luck," Tessie answered, "and I had the full consent of my husband."

It was more than a quarter of a century ago when Tessie Valdez had her first extra-marital love affair. She was on vacation in her province Cagayan, when she met this young mother with 7 children and a husband who was very poor and out of work. She fell in love with the couple's 6-month old baby girl named Noemi Cardenas. "Let me adopt her, raise her to be a nice girl and send her to school," she said to the parents who were only too glad to have one child that may be the only one in the family to have an education.

It was hard to raise this girl, so a few years later, Tessie adopted another girl, Alicia Borja, who was already 9 years old, to keep Noemi company. Both girls grew up together. But Noemi, only 3rd year high school, fell in love and ran away, and became pregnant. Tessie took her back, forced her to finish high school and secretarial course, and put her to work in Daiichi Densi Electronics. Noemi is now 26 years old, married to her old boyfriend, but her first child was adopted by Tessie. Alicia Borja obediently finished her high school too, got married, and at 25 years of age, has three children, one of whom was also adopted by Tessie.

The two little boys of Noemi and Alicia grew up together with the love and care of Tessie Valdez. In addition to those two, she also adopted the son of her own son, Arturo Jr., an engineer from Mapua, now 36 years old and in business. Arturo's son, Arnel Valdez is 7 years old and is in grade one; Noemi's Manuel Luis Cardenas is 11 years of age and is in Grade 5; Alicia's Romulo Japonete is 8 years of age and is in Grade Two. These three little boys are still in Tessie's care, her own personal Three Musketeers.

As if these are not enough, Tessie fell in love once more with a little girl one year and 2 months old named Elizabeth Abobo, a child of impoverished parents in Pangasinan. She persuaded the parents to let her adopt the child. And she did, sending her all the way through high school and the secretarial course. Elizabeth was working at Dynetics when she got involved with a pen pal in Australia. She wanted to see him so she hired herself out as domestic help to some Australian family, went to Melbourne, met the guy, accepted his proposal and dragged him back here to be married in church, just so Tessie Valdez and the rest of the family can attend. Today, she is 28 years old, and lives in Melbourne, Australia, as Mrs. Glenn MacKenzie. Tessie is really proud of this girl, *"Mabait talaga!"*

Another child Tessie is proud of is Revelina Caliba whom she assisted as a teenager of 15 years, sending her to nursing school, till at last Revelina found employment as a nurse in a hospital in Switzerland. At the age of 29 years, she is another source of pride and of precious dollars, *"Mabait Talaga!"*

One day, Tessie Valdez, going to the Pasay Market, saw a little boy sleeping on the sidewalk. She asked him where his parents were, and he said he did not even know his parents. Here he was, Jose Apostol, 8 years of age, full of skin afflictions (sarna), dirty, starved and lonely, without any one in the whole world who cared about him. And Tessie Valdez fell in love with him, took him home, gave him a bath, a bed, a place to call home. She sent him to school, even if he did not enjoy studying, right through high school. He broke her heart by eloping with the laundry woman. He is now 36 years old, and she loves him still.

The nice thing about Tessie's love affairs is that she encourages her adopted children to visit, love, and help their natural parents. The capacity to love is indeed infinitely infinite, if one has a heart like that of Tessie Valdez.

Reader, have you paid something of the cost of poverty, ignorance and injustice? Yes you have, and you are not through paying. For in this way and that, for the rest of your days, the cost will appear.

It will appear in the form of deductions from your paycheck, taxes you have to pay to support a colonial bureaucracy of unemployable incompetents.

It will appear in the insistent tug on your shirtsleeves and your heart-strings for a little coin and sympathy.

It will appear in the high walls you build and the guards you hire to protect your homes.

It will appear in the anonymous faces that might have been those of your loved ones, faces in the newspapers that scream of rape, prostitution, hate and violence.

Or it will appear, as it does to Teresita Valdez of Cagayan, in the bright and shining faces of coming generations, in love and faith and hope for the future, in ideals that live within her and through her unto her issue -- there to multiply a thousand, a million times fold, till they sweep across the land and shape the destiny of our nation.

August 10, 1986

Part 2. To be Poor

My father used to say, "I have been broke many times, but I have never been poor. To be poor is a state of mind, of hopelessness, of helplessness. To be poor is to lose faith in one's self."   Like my father I have never been poor, but I never really knew what being poor means until I read Conrad de Quiros' essay on *Tongues on Fire*, excerpts of which I shall quote and paraphrase in the rest of this article. Conrad wrote:

You just stray one street away from your house, and you would not just step into another neighborhood, you would slip into another world. The poverty and violence and wretchedness are right where you stand. They are another city entirely, the sense that Charles Dickens used the phrase in "A Tale of Two Cities."

This is a world where a dozen people squeeze into space separated from the next one by cardboards, tin cans, and the aluminum posters and election streamers! -- and still manage to have a love life, which is why they are dozen in the first place. This is a world where garbage has turned into a mountain, blocking out sun and air and hope.

This is a world where taxi drivers are knifed to death in the dark of night for a thousand bucks, the murderers sobbing when they are caught that they needed the money to buy medicine for a child that was sick and dying.

I once read about how a man killed his family and committed suicide. The man had been jobless for some time, a fact that had led to his wife and brood of six children going hungry. Not one of the children was old enough to help put food on the table, and it was all his wife could do to cook and wash clothes and take care of the kids. Which left the burden of keeping the family's body and soul together solely on him. He was often seen talking to himself in a corner. On the fateful day, he came home in high spirits. Their problems, he told his family, were over. He did not say how, his eyes merely gleamed with a maniacal light. That night, he mixed insecticide in the gruel they had for supper. And before long, they were groveling and vomiting all over the floor.

The kids went first, turning blue in the face and choking to death. The wife went last, scrambling frantically to the side of the kids who were writhing in pain when her husband's diabolical plot finally dawned on her before she herself blacked out. She was brought to the hospital but they could not bring her back. She probably did not want to come back.

To be poor is to be assailed by impossibility
I did hear when I was in Bangladesh some years ago about a man who also murdered his family after his wife decided to pawn her nose ring. To him, nothing could come lower, nothing could speak more of his utter unworthiness to be a husband and father. The Filipino himself who murdered his wife and kids had been heard to say he could no longer sleep, the sobs and whimpers of his kids while they wasted away before his eyes bore through his brain like mosquitoes buzzing crazily in the ears. He had become nothing, he had become less than nothing.

Of course, not all the poor commit suicide in the face of seeming hopelessness, any more than they become sex performers as a result of it.

Not all the poor reach such depths of madness. This is a strange country where poor people perform sex as a way out of poverty.

There is a true divide between rich and poor. To be rich is to be replete with possibility. You may not have money in your pockets and still be rich. To be rich is to know that nothing is impossible. To be rich is to know that you can go around any obstacle, go under or over any obstacle, go through any obstacle. It is to know that when you want money, you can lay your hands on it. It is to know that when you need people, you can get in touch with them. It is to know that when you want something done, you can get it done.

To be poor on the other hand, is to be assailed by impossibility. It is to be thwarted at every turn' It is to have obstacle after obstacle put in your path until you no longer see the goal, until you no longer know there is a goal, until you learn only to toil to get past the obstacle you wake up to each day at crack of dawn. It is quite literally to have no one to turn to.

Not the family heaving their sighs at the other side of the cardboard box, not the brother or father who are themselves shrilly issuing cries for help, certainly not the government or bank official who cannot understand why in this world of endless alternatives, you cannot find a job or livelihood to get you past your despair.

To be poor is to be in the lower deck of a ship of fools
We hear the phrase, "empowering the people" or "empowering the poor," who are in fact most of the people. Those who try to make this possible say that the poor have been gagged, and that if you can only remove the muzzle that keeps their mouths shut, they would send their powerful shouts to heaven.

But what if the poor have lost their voice altogether? What if the knifing of taxi drivers for a thousand bucks, the keening of hungry children like dogs at the scent of death, or the pitiless decision to embrace the comfort of death for oneself and for one's loved ones, are the signs of a cavernous muteness?

Most Filipinos live that way today. In the lower deck of this ship of state, or ship of fools.

How to talk to them? What language to communicate to the voiceless, to those who have lost the capacity to cry out from the pit of their lungs, or souls? I don't know.

I am no longer young, and though I have not lost a great deal of my energies, I have lost a great deal of my certainties. I can only guess that the first step is a change of attitude. To be able to talk to the human cargo, or derelicts, in the lower deck, you should first want to. It is at least a testament to Rizal as witness his days in Dapitan, that he was willing to break bread with the *masa*.

That is not as easy as it seems, in the case of a real boat. I have been to one, way back in the late 1970s. It added new dimensions of meaning to the phrase "floating coffins." Habitation in the third class consisted of wooden bunks piled in rows, one on top of another, like the tiers of the dead in La Loma Cemetery, with nearly exactly the same amount of height between them. There was only little more than space for a casket, or for your chest to rise and fall with each breath. To get to your bunk, you had to weave through a tangle of callused arms and legs and famished bodies strewn below. Each time I hear about a boat that sunk in the waters between these islands, I see that sight again, and shudder.

To be poor is to be invisible

It is not easy to want to go down to the lower deck of the boat. The sight and the smell assail you from the very top of the stairs, like the vapor from a parched earth at the first patter of rain. Society's answer to that problem in fact has been to make the people in the lower deck disappear completely. It has been to make them invisible. People who were there but were not there. People who served but were not observed, people who spoke but were not heard, people who existed but were not seen.

Invisible men are what Filipinos are in the heart of this country. Or invisible women, as the women's groups are bound to insist, women living even more ghostly lives than men in this country. They are the shadowy figures that surround us but which we cannot see. They are the strands of insubstantial matter that float around us, but which we cannot catch.

They are the emaciated forms that lie on the sidewalks at night, finding temporary refuge through the deadly fumes of *rugby* contact cement, whom we pass by but acknowledge in the same way that we acknowledge the pavement to be there. They are the blotches we see through the rain, tapping on the windows of our cars with scrawny fingers, whom we flip coins to and roll the glass rapidly down on not so much to avoid getting wet but to avoid looking at their faces.

Everywhere, the institutions of society conspire to hide them from sight. The Church does so by turning them into a radiant flock, filling up the churches in their Sunday best, their eyes turned heavenward in blissful supplication, laughing without joy at the thought of salvation.

In movies, the poor caught in the clutches of desperation copulate without shame in front of an audience. Imelda used to put up huge billboards of her nutrition program on the road used by visiting dignitaries to hide the hovels that lay in the path of their vision.

Government makes the poor invisible in a similar way. "On this site," say the billboards that hide the jagged roofs made from biscuit cans, "will rise the new Philippines." The poor are no longer the tangle of arms and legs and the mass of frail bodies we must blot out on our way to our mansions, they are a statistical aggregate that has been temporarily disadvantaged, dis-empowered, and inconvenienced. But not for long. Economic growth will eradicate poverty, even if it has to eradicate the poor.

Talking to the poor in their own language
The media make them invisible even as they transfix them into very visible corpses that float on the river, or headless bodies that rot in iron drums. The charitable institutions make them invisible even as they transform them into very bottomless pits resembling human bellies into which are poured food and medicine, alms for the body and balms for the soul. Even the poor themselves make them invisible even they materialize from the fog of invisibility to become maids and nurses and forklift operators in strange lands.

The last I caught a glimpse of when a group of OFWs in Singapore protested the airing of Probe Team in Singapore on the ground that it was giving their country a bad name. The TV program had featured among others rampant pedophilia in Pagsanjan, fraternity hazing in the University of the Philippines, and the mountain of garbage that had buried the folk of Payatas. Why couldn't the program show the country in a better light? -- they asked.

We want to pin down the gaseous vapors that suffuse us daily, which we breathe like air, or contract like virus. We have to discover the magic wand that makes their atoms come together and integrate them into solid matter. We want to talk to them, discover before our impetuous anger stokes their resentments into a revolutionary flame.

There is one other thing we have to do if we want to talk to the human flotsam that occupies the lower deck of this boat. It is to want to speak their language.

It's not as easy too as it seems. I often wonder, in our time, if the elections themselves are not our way of saying that if the poor want to talk to us, or at all, they must speak our language. I know that I applauded the efforts of the television networks and various groups to help voters vote wisely. But I don't know that that really strikes at the heart of the matter. Voter education campaigns do help to show voters how to vote wisely. They do not help to show the poor why they should.

Why should the poor vote wisely? Why should the poor vote at all? Why should the insubstantial shadows that flit around us that we do not see take elections as though they were the air they breathe? Why should they enjoy the electoral love-making – like the sex on a cramped mat among the sleeping children, that they take refuge in? You are a spouse or lover, would you easily melt into the arms of someone who ignores you or disappears from your life for months on end and suddenly materializes from out of nowhere with a rose in one hand a bottle of wine on the other demanding to get a lay in the hay? The only difference being that the candidates do not disappear for months from their lives, they disappear for years.

Bridging the gap between rich and poor

We call the poor dumb for not voting wisely, which is just another way of saying for not voting the way we want them to. Isn't that a little like calling the spouse or lover you treat like dirt, or the thing you push hurriedly away after love-making, a whore for preferring the charms of more attentive politicians whom you consider undeserving suitors?

If the poor are what I've said they are, elections themselves take on the aspect of giving cake to the hungry. If the poor are what I've said they are, pointing out to them the differential parliamentary virtues of candidates takes on the aspect of pointing to those who need bread the differential dietary properties of cakes. If the poor are what I've said they are, even appealing to their parental instincts to think about the future of their children, takes on the aspect of appealing to the desperate to keep the cakes fossilized in the cupboard so that their more civilizable children will have the chance to appreciate culinary properties one day.

A friend of mine, an American journalist, once gave me to see just what elections mean for poor folk. She said, in Kampuchea, but it might as well be the Philippines, asked what she thought about elections, one old woman answered very thoughtfully: "Well, it's obvious the elections didn't work the first time. That's why we're having them again."

Given all this, the tempting course is just to keep to the upper deck, where the breezes blow and the wine flows, where the sun shines on those who speak English and Spanish and fill them with a glow. The tempting course is just to speak the language of the cosmopolite, the language of globalization, the language of power and domination, and insist that the disjointed bodies below somehow manage to shuffle their feet to their beat.

But that is the reason this country has never been able to understand itself. We want heal that rift, we want to bridge that gap, we have to reconstruct atom by atom, strand by strand, sinew by sinew, the tenuous mass that has melted in the dark below till it becomes distinguishable, living and breathing human forms. We want to mend the break, we want to glue the tear, we have to piece together, word by word, syntax by syntax, meaning by meaning, the indecipherable whispers and loud bellowing issuing from the pit below till they assemble themselves into something resembling speech. We want to stop the alienation, we have to rip off plank by plank, beam by beam, ballast by ballast, the thing that divides this ship of state, or ship of fools, into upper and lower decks till we commonly feel the rush of wind and smell the briny water.

And then maybe, just maybe, one day we might leave this ship a little wiser for having been there.

May 17-24, 2001

Part 3. Was it a Cebuano who first circumnavigated the world?

Was it Ferdinand Magellan or Sebastian del Cano or Enrique, a Cebuano, who was the first man to circle the globe? Historian Ambeth Ocampo bewails the fact that our children are being asked to memorize historical facts as if they were part of the TV game Trivial Pursuit, and they are so often wrong. Magellan is often identified as a Spaniard because he served the Spanish king. He is not, he is a Portuguese subject. Ambeth also recalls that a frequent error is saying "circumcision" of the globe, instead of "circumnavigate."

In Spanish history books, the first man to circumnavigate the globe was Sebastian del Cano, who left Spain with Ferdinand Magellan and was the captain of Victoria, the vessel that was able to complete the voyage back to Spain. Magellan left Spain with 270 men, and del Cano was one of 18 men who made it back. Every one of the 18 should have shared the glory but del Cano was captain, so it was he who was honored by King Carlos V, and given a coat of arms with a globe and an inscription that said "*Primus circumdidisti me* (You are first to circumnavigate me)."

But Antonio Pigafetta, the chronicler of the Magellan expedition, who authored the book "The First Voyage Around the World" failed to mention Sebastian del Cano as such, because del Cano joined a mutiny which Magellan suppressed. Had the mutiny succeeded, del Cano might not have been given the honor.

Portuguese historians insist that *Ferdinand Magellan* is the first circumnavigator, because although he died in Mactan, he previously took the eastern route to Molucca in the East Indies about the same longitude as the Philippines, then returned to Spain. He later took the western route across the Altantic and the Pacific and died in the Philippines, thereby completing a full circle, although the route between the Molucca and the Philippines was not covered.

Now our historian, my uncle Carlos Quirino, made international news by pointing out that according the Pigafetta, in Molucca, Magellan picked up an interpreter whom he called Enrique whom he brought back to Spain, then back to the Philippines. Enrique was able to communicate with Cebuanos in their own language. Quirino speculates that most probably

Enrique came from Cebu, and was brought in his youth to Molucca. Thus he was able to complete the voyage from the Philippines back to the Philippines, a full circle around the globe.

White historians were unkind to Enrique whom they called Black Henry because he was involved in the murder of some survivors of the Battle of Mactan who were killed by Cebuanos during a party. Enrique is most probably a Cebuano because he would not join the Cebuano resistance otherwise. So Enrique is not only the first circumnavigator but also joins Lapu-Lapu as a one of the first freedom fighters against the Spaniards.

A film maker named Eric de Guia who calls himself Kidlat Tahimik, a friend of mine, who lives in Baguio, is said to have made a film on the life of Enrique. That would be something interesting to watch.

December 14, 1994

Part 4. Snow-White's Seven Dwarfs: The Jesuit Mafia

Ninoy Aquino never even knew they existed, for they surfaced only after that tragic day in August 1983. Today they are the most powerful group within the Cory Aquino Administration, and they stand against what Ninoy and the opposition long stood for: Nationalism, Economic Independence, Industrialization and Self-Reliance.

In the platforms of Unido and Salonga's Liberal Party, in the Underlying Principles of the Convenors' Group, even in the Declaration of Common Principles of the United Opposition submitted by Ninoy to the Solarz Committee two months before he was killed, one promise stood out: independence from the impositions of IMF and multinational corporations. And that is what this new group is precisely against.

Jimmy's Cronies

They are called the Jesuit Mafia, and without fanfare, they have taken over twelve of the most important positions in Cory's administration; PDP-Laban and its political allies can count on six; Laurel's Unido has four; and the Human Rights group has four.

Well, count it out: (1) Jaime Ongpin for Finance; (2) Jose Concepcion for Trade & Industry; (3) Lourdes Quisumbing for Education; (4) Jose Antonio Gonzalez for Tourism; (5) Alfredo Bengzon for Health; (6) Teodoro Locsin Jr. for Public Information;

(7) Solita Monsod for NEDA; (8) Jose Fernandez for Central Bank Governor; (9) Vicente Jayme, President of the PNB; (10) Cesar Zalamea, Chairman of DBP; (11) Bienvenido Tan of BIR; and (12) Jose Cuisia of SSS. These are also known as Jimmy's Cronies, the Jesuit-Ateneo-Harvard-IMF-AmCham Mafiosi.

Add to this the 13th member of the Jesuit Cosa Nostra, Aquilino Pimentel, Minister of Local Governments, who is tapped to be the next president of the Philippines by the Jesuit and the Americans, and who also is the chairman of PDP-Laban.

PDP-Laban and its Convenor affiliates have in addition: Neptali Gonzalez for Justice; Ramon Mitra for Agriculture; Jovito Salonga, for Good Government; Jose Diokno for Human Rights; Teofisto Guingona, for Audit. With Nene Pimentel, that's six all in all.

The Human Rights group from the MABINI has Joker Arroyo as Executive Secretary; Rene Saguisag as Presidential Spokesman; Bobbit Sanchez for Labor; and Antonio Carpio for National Bureau of Investigation. That's four.

The Unido and the NUC have only Salvador Laurel for Foreign Affairs; Ernesto Maceda for Natural Resources and Energy; Luis Villafuerte for Government Reorganization; and Alberto Romulo for Budget. That's four. Doy Laurel complains and blames the PDP-Laban for squeezing him out, but he is barking up the wrong tree.

Aside from Jose Diokno who is with the Convenor's Group, the only one of the Nationalist group in the government is Wigberto Tañada in the Bureau of Customs. Nationalists who fought the longest against President Marcos, like Senator Lorenzo Tañada, Alejandro Roces, Alejandro Lichauco, Homobono Adaza, Agapito Aquino, Charito Planas, and Heherson Alvarez.

The Seven Dwarfs

During the political campaign, while everyone else was in the streets getting their heads blown off, and on the political platforms shouting themselves hoarse, a group headed by Ateneo president Joaquin Bernas SJ, and Jaime Ongpin were meeting daily on the 7th floor of the Cojuangco Building. No one was allowed to join them or disturb them, but they were rumored to have spent the better part of the day in prayer and marching around the conference table singing "Hi-Ho, Hi-Ho, it's off to work we go!" That's why they were called Snow-White's (or Cory's) Seven Dwarfs.

Father Bernas the leader was of course Doc; and bad-tempered Jimmy Ongpin was called Grumpy; Ramon del Rosario Jr., because of his chinky eyes was called Sleepy; Alran Bengson was Sneezy; Peping Cojuangco was called Bashful; good-looking and ebullient Teddy Boy Locsin was Happy; and Noel Soriano, who was after all not an Atenean but Father Delaney's boy in the U.P. Catholic Action, was left with the appellation Dopey.

According to Dopey, the Seven Dwarfs were "coordinating" the entire campaign. Which probably means acting as a liaison between Cory and the Makati Business Club (which is controlled by the Multinationals and the Opus Dei); acting as a conduit for much needed funds from the MBC, and dispenser of such necessities as helicopters and safe-houses; and above all taking charge of the re-education of Cory Aquino as a Defender of the Faith and of American interests.

This re-education of Cory consisted of getting suggested drafts for Cory's speeches from many sources, and re-writing them to purge the final draft of anything that is remotely pro-Filipino or offensive to the Americans and the IMF. Grumpy himself would get Cory to attend a seminar of Opus Dei economists in Singapore in the company of no less than Bosworth's informant and favorite economist Bernardo Villegas and side-kick Jesus Estanislao -- who are known as Hans and Fritz, the Katzenjammer Kids of CRC, partly because they are financed by the neo-fascist Hans Seidel Stiftung of Bavaria.

Grumpy is the Real President

Grumpy divulged that he was given a "free hand" to handle the economy and the government financial institutions, and that gives him more power than Virata ever had. His hand is controlling policies concerning Education, Tourism, Public Information, and tax collection, as well. He is the only one who can keep in office the discredited minions of the previous administration (like Cesar Zalamea), and the colleagues of Marcos' cronies such as Jesus Estanislao, consultant of Kokoy Romualdez's PCI Bank and columnist of Kokoy's Makati/Binondo Business Times, in addition to Bernie Villegas whose brother Jose agitated the Hacienda Luisita tenants and picketed Cory's residence. And Grumpy uses his power to keep out anyone who does not agree with him.

You see, Grumpy like his brother Bobby Ongpin, does not really believe in the policy of "consultation, not dictation" of President Aquino. When Enriquito Zobel opted to support Marcos, all reasonable men said "The damn fool does not know what he is talking about, but he is entitled to his opinion." But not Grumpy who said, "I am quitting the Makati Business Club until Enriquito is not longer its chairman." Poor Enriquito is simply exiled from the company of Grumpy, because Grumpy just hates to argue with anyone who disagrees with him, in addition to being *pikon* or onion-skinned about criticisms. Grumpy would make it a condition for his acceptance of the Finance portfolio that CB Governor Jobo Fernandez be retained; that he be given "free hand" and absolute powers to handle the economy along with government financial institutions like DBP, PNB, GSIS and SSS, as well as government corporations like PAL and Manila Hotel; that no appointments are made without "prior consultation" with him. And if he does not get what he wants, he gets into a terrible tantrum, and makes *sumbong* to the American Embassy.

On constitutional questions, Ministers Pimentel and Neptali Gonzalez are counterbalanced by Ms. Cecilia Palma and Homobono Adaza; on questions of subversion and military abuse, Enrile and Ramos are counterbalanced by the MABINI group of Saguisag and Joker Arroyo. But in the economic field, Grumpy stands alone and unopposed; none is allowed to question, to moderate, to argue the nationalist position in the face of what is perceived to be a complete and unconditional surrender to the IMF and the multinational corporations.

This makes Grumpy in effect the real President of the Philippines without being elected, propelled into power with nothing except the support of the American Embassy and the IMF, the same guys who put Cesar Virata, Vicente Valdepeñas and Bobby Ongpin into power in the Marcos Administration and plunged our nation into bankruptcy and economic depression. God help us now.

March. 18, 1986

Part 5. Eulogy For Ninoy Aquino
When on April 14, 1865, Abraham Lincoln was assassinated, his

biographer and great poet Carl Sandburg compared him to a great oak standing on top of a hill suddenly felled by a lightning stroke. He wrote:

> *Did any lover of trees*
> *Have a daybreak dream*
> *Of a Great Oak on a high hill,*
> *Under the flash of a lightning prong*
> *Crashing down helpless –*
> *A loss for all time*
> *To the winds and the sky who had loved it,*
> *And had not known how much they loved it...*

Like the Great Oak on the high hill, Ninoy Aquino is gone forever, and like the winds and the sky, we who love him feel an incalculable sense of loss. But a tree is best measured when it is down. And now is time to evaluate the legacy Ninoy Aquino handed down to those of us he left behind.

I remember with fondness when I first met Ninoy. I was the Chairman of the National Economic Council, and Ninoy was the newly elected Governor of Tarlac. He came to see me for two reasons. First he came with maps to show that the American government was buying enormous tracts of land in Tarlac, and he wanted me to get the President to get assurance from the American Ambassador that they are not going to set up a missile base in the Philippines. Second, Ninoy wanted to offer Tarlac as the project area for a Foreign Aid program utilizing rebuilt road building equipment from Japan. I told him he's too late, I already signed an agreement with Laguna upon the advice of my staff. He laughed and said that nationalist that I am, I must have chosen Laguna because it was the province of Jose Rizal. I laughingly admitted it, and Ninoy coyly suggested, "How about the province of Jose Rizal's greatest love, Leonor Rivera? Surely, as a nationalist and a lover, you cannot keep Rizal and his Love apart." How could I refuse? Tarlac became a Project Area, and I never regretted it, since Ninoy's success encouraged him to leave the Nationalista party and join the Liberal Party, about the same time Ferdinand Marcos turned from Liberal to Nacionalista. Fair exchange, I thought.

Ninoy's life has always been an exaggeration. While most of us attended only one school, he attended four. He studied in La Salle, Ateneo, San Beda and the University of the Philippines.

If he had time I am sure, he would have enrolled in U.S.T. as well, because he wanted to have as many classmates and schoolmates as possible. But unfortunately, he did not have the time. At the age of 17, when most of us are just preparing for the Junior Prom, Ninoy was already a full-fledged war correspondent in Korea. A year later he went to the mountains and convinced the Communist Supremo Luis Taruc to surrender to the authorities. He was the youngest mayor, the youngest governor, and the youngest senator ever to be elected. We run together as senatorial aspirants, Ninoy and I, the in company of Camilo Osias, Soc Rodrigo and Maria Kalaw Katigbak. Ninoy was elected with such a majority of votes, he was the only one Marcos could not cheat.

Ninoy had always been in the center of historical events, not only in the Philippines but also in the rest of the world. He was in Korea as a newspaperman and was decorated for it. When the French surrendered to the Vietnam forces in Dienbienphu, he was there. In Guatemala, he witnessed the assassination of President Castillo-Armas by CIA agent Pol Valeriano, a Filipino expatriate who was the husband of Emma Araneta who is the mother of Greggy Araneta, who is the husband of Irene Marcos who is the daughter of Ferdinand Marcos, who is the husband of Imelda. In Sumatra, during the Colonel's Revolt against President Sukarno of Indonesia, he was there to witness the secret role of the CIA using Philippine bases to supply arms to the rebels. I thought I was one of the first Filipinos to enter Red China, but when I got there, Ninoy was there before me, knocking at the doors of North Vietnam from mainland China.

I have no doubt that if Ninoy Aquino had become our President, he would have been a great world leader as well, leading the Third World Nations against the impositions of the imperialistic nations and the communist world. Ninoy Aquino was in the center of history, but he was also in the embrace of posterity. How else can we explain why 60% of those who mourn him, hardly knew him, and were barely in Grade One when Martial Law was declared. Yet Ninoy is the idol of the Youth as no one else can claim. Let me recount a story that may explain this phenomenon. Some 16 years ago when my second-born son whose name is Atom...A for Alfredo, Tom for Tomas, Atom BUM, we call him... was only 14 years of age, I brought him with me on one of my meetings with Ninoy. Lo and behold, Ninoy and Atom were in deep conversation. Feeling left out, I inquired what they were talking about. Ninoy answered, "We are talking about a subject you may not be interested in... the politics of La Salle Green Hills. Didn't you know your son Atom is running for the Student Council next week? He just appointed me his campaign manager." I thought Ninoy was joking, but a few days later, I saw Atom distributing literature with pictures of both Ninoy and Atom, with captions quoting Ninoy as Senator of the Republic endorsing Atom for the La Salle Student Council. On the day of the election, there was pandemonium in La Salle when Ninoy's helicopter landed in the football field, and Ninoy himself emerged with a bullhorn, saying, "This is Ninoy Aquino, the campaign manager of Atom Henares. I am leaving my helicopter here the whole day. Those who vote for Atom may have a helicopter ride around Manila, which takes only five minutes. Come on boys, here's your chance to spit on Ateneo." Atom of course won overwhelmingly. I kidded Ninoy about what I deemed a childish caper. He laughed but his answer was serious, "Larry, Atom is more important than you and me, he is our future. Whatever I do for you will be forgotten tomorrow. But what I just did for Atom will be remembered long after I am gone, by Atom, by all his friends, by all La Salle, and through the grapevine by all the youth in Manila and the Philippines." No wonder the Youth loved Ninoy. And Atom, now a 30-year-old president of a large corporation, shed tears for days at Ninoy's residence, at Sto. Domingo Church, through every step of the 10-hour procession to Manila Memorial Park. Ninoy was right, everyone remembered. A Titan had walked in our midst. When comes such another?

Passionate, yet never fanatic, coldly analytical while being provocative, traditional without being conservative, progressive without being radical, Ninoy embraced the cause of Nationalism and Democracy in our nation's darkest hour, arousing the unforgiving rancor, the brooding hatred, the lasting enmity of the powers-that- be. He did not care. He could afford not to care. For in an acquisitive society where status is fixed by wealth, he inherited, married and acquired more than he needed and was never corrupted by greed. In a society hypnotized by slogans and dogmas, he had a mind of his own and the courage to speak it out. In a conformist society, he was a dissenter. In a frivolous society, he was a thinker and doer. In the Philippine zoo with its exhibitionist monkeys, cowardly coyotes, idle peacocks, trained parrots and predatory hawks, Ninoy Aquino was an uncaged lion. Judge him by the enemies he made! His enemies were Apathy, Timidity, Servility; Opportunism in a coat and tie; Hypocrisy in a barong tagalog; Ambition, Intolerance, Greed; Poverty, Ignorance, Injustice; and above all TYRANNY --- he fought them all, and he was proud of his wounds!

May it not be said that Ninoy Aquino lived for a lost cause, that he was, as someone said, an outsider to his own generation. May it not be said that he spent himself in a meaningless battle, to save a nation that refuses to save itself. If the cause of Philippine democracy died with Ninoy Aquino, then by God, it deserves to die.

Who then shall take his place? A number of public figures come to mind, but they all seem sadly inadequate. History has a way of resolving these anxieties. The day Burgos, Gomez and Zamora were garroted to the general dismay of the population, no one could have guessed that in an obscure town called Calamba, a precocious eleven-year old boy, whose mother had been imprisoned unjustly by a Spanish official, would be so horrified by the bloody deed in Manila and by the subsequent persecutions against an elder brother Paciano that he would determine to give his life to his people's vindication; or that another lad, even younger and considerably less fortunate, perhaps sleepless that night with the pangs of starvation, lay back in his hovel in Tondo mesmerized by the idea of the Katipunan! Or that the brilliant valiant band of propagandists, soldiers and patriots were to be, in the moment of their country's greatest need, just where they had to be to best serve her. Also on that bleak December morn, when it was Jose Rizal's turn, the weeping multitudes could not have known of the destiny of the young boy Quezon or that of a small child, only six years old, Claro M. Recto, who would do their best to take the place of those who had "fallen in the night".

Even as we mourn the passing of Ninoy Aquino, some fledgling politician in a distant *municipio* is perhaps already in the throes of patriotic idealism, or some callow teenager sickened and outraged by our times, is already poring over his plans for our salvation. He may have been walking in the funeral procession, he may even be among you out there, listening to me, and carrying

his fate and ours in his whirling burning brain.
Sto. Tomas University, Sept. 15, 1983

Part 6. The story behind the Mimosa deal

Antonio Gonzalez is accusing the Erap Administration officials, principally Flagship Projects Secretary Robert Aventajado of cheating him out of his Mimosa company, offering to testify in the Impeachment Trial of President Erap Estrada. Who is Antonio Gonzalez??

Tony Gonzalez belongs to the Pangasinan clan which originally owned the Pantranco transportation empire. Adman Dindo Gonzalez who propelled Ramon Magsaysay to the presidency, Ambassador Luis Gonzalez, first husband of Vicky Quirino, as well as Beauty Queen Margie Moran, are his relatives. He doesn't speak Pangasinense, but a peculiar kind of Spanish spoken only by the coño boys of La Salle. He is a playboy whom we call Speedy Gonzalez (*andale, andale!*) who married the niece of the late Dr. Carlos Sevilla, left her for a morena beauty who in turn left him for Atong Ang. Speedy Gonzalez was one of the first contributors to the Cory political campaign and was awarded the position of Tourism Secretary by which he set up the Duty Free stores to compete with local industries. He owned the Mondragon firm which appropriately enough sells brassieres and women's accessories, and it was managed for him by my first cousin Dulce Saguisag (wife of Rene) who eventually replaced Gloria Macapagal Arroyo in the Erap Cabinet. But that is another story. My cousin Dulce is a professional social worker who has been considered for the Social Welfare portfolio many times before since Cory's time but managed again and again to be displaced by political appointees. She will stay there up to the end of December.

During the Ramos Administration Speedy Gonzalez was able to acquire the golf club and hotel facilities of the Clark Military Base, as well as a franchise to operate a casino – a tourist facility which was named Mimosa. The failure of the government to build an international airport in Clark Field and a railroad link to Metro Manila, as well as the cancellation of the Centennial Celebrations centered on Clark Field, resulted in the near bankruptcy of Mimosa.

By the time the Erap Administration came into power, Mimosa was already being foreclosed by the Clark Development Corporation and the Pagcor for failure to live up to its obligations and for unpaid debts of about P4 billion. Venicio "Boy" Ramos, son of Teofilo Ramos, number two man in the Iglesia Ni Cristo hierarchy, was the conduit for a deal to bail out Mimosa. Penta Capital, owned by Opus Dei banker Jovino Cinco, offered to buy the majority stock of Mimosa and make available P600 million cash to the beleaguered company.

The deal was to be approved by the Clark Development and the Office of the President. Venicio Ramos recommended to Tony that he engage Robert Aventajado to clinch the deal and get the approval of President Erap Estrada for an amended contract with the Clark Development. It was beauty queen Margie Moran who arranged the first meeting of Tony Gonzalez and Robert. In that meeting Robert advised Tony to procure the services of a law firm, Agabin Law Office, to draft the memorandum of agreement for submission to the Clark Development Corporation and approval of a new lease agreement by the Office of the President.

The Contract of Lease for the Clark Field facilities was allegedly disadvantageous to the government. The first agreement stipulated a lease payment of P72 billion in 30 years. The amended agreement stipulated a lease payment of only P4 billion in 30 years. The Agapin Law firm was found to be headed by an aunt of Robert Aventajado, and held office on the same floor and next door to the Aventajado's offices on the 6th floor of Pacific Star Building. All the offices were rented from William Gatchalian, alleged Presidential crony, presidential adviser on Overseas Contract Workers by virtue of having donated a million pesos to Rosa Malabanan.

William, originally from Hong Kong was once accused by Jose Diokno of having bribed his way to Filipino citizenship for himself and his nine brothers and sisters in the 1960s, and in the 1980s. William was accused by then Secretary of Justice Franklin Drilon of massive smuggling of plastic materials, and of mysteriously getting the Bureau of Customs to cause to disappear the entire file of all his import papers. Of his 1,600 shipments, not a single import paper was left in the files, only tracers as they were moved from one place to another. For a long time, stories were rife about plastic materials brought in tax-free under the bonded manufacturing warehouse, to be shipped out again as finished products for export. Instead container vans filled with rocks were shipped to Japan and dumped into the sea.

Tony accuses Robert Aventajado of having demanded and received 20 percent goodwill contribution which Tony paid to the Millennium Holdings, owned by Joey Antonio, in which Robert's son is Vice-President. Robert claims his son is "on the job" training as part of his education. This is probably the first time in the whole history of education in this country where an on-the job training is given not to student apprentices, but to the son of a highly placed official, for the high post of Vice President.

Thus Tony Speedy Gonzalez lost his Mimosa firm to the Penta Capital of Opus Dei Jovino Cinco, and to the Millennium Holdings of Joey Antonio and Robert Aventajado's son. If I were Speedy Gonzalez I wouldn't volunteer to testify against President Erap Estrada in the Impeachment Trial. His accusations have very weak links to Aventajado, and much less to the President. Other accusations against the president have better credence and bolstered by more credible evidence.

December 21-22, 2000

Part 7. Opus Dei aims for the Commission of Audit!

Jose Cremades, remember that name. It is the name of one of the most powerful men in the Philippines. He is a Spanish Catholic priest who really believes that God Almighty is exclusively at the service of the Opus Dei and no one else. He is the real power behind the local Opus Dei, and as such he has absolute control over the minds and souls of such Opus Dei diehards as economist/educator Bernie Villegas with his decorticated sconce, ex-Finance Secretary Jesus Estanislao with his balding pate, the Son of Sun ex-Central Bank Governor Jose Cuisia, Metro Bank Chairman Cidito Mapa. His "spiritual directors" demand that Opus Dei members reveal the details of every sin they commit without the protection of the seal of confession, thus exposing them to the most cruel blackmail and exploitation if they step out of line, as Esteban Latorre did.

Jose Cremades is a dark brooding Spaniard of a modern Holy Inquisition, which makes him in the most awesome and most ominous sense of the term a Great White Father to those of us with a colonial mentality. Obsessed in the pursuit of wealth and power, just as the Opus Dei was during the dictatorship of General Francisco Franco in Spain and of General Augusto Pinochet in Chile, his Opus Dei secretive organization has extended its tentacles into every nook and corner of business, media and government in the administration of Erap Estrada.

He is not missing any bets. His supernumerary Atty. Pancho Villaraza, law partner of Tony Carpio and associate of General Jose Almonte, has latched on as financier and adviser to Vice-President Gloria Macapagal Arroyo. And as shown in TV clips, Joey Cuisia, Cidito Mapa and Gary Teves have joined Gloria's bandwagon, without ever being part of the parliament of the streets (as they refused to be in Edsa).

But Father Jose Cremades is playing his greatest cards with Erap. His Kit Tatad is going all out for Erap in the Impeachment Trial. For some time now his numerary Dodo Mandanas, erstwhile right-hand man of Imelda Marcos in the Department of Human Settlements, and one time bidder for the Lotto contract, has been actively campaigning, aided by Raul de Guzman whose wife and daughters are of the Opus Dei, to be appointed as the new Chief of the Commission on Audit when the incumbent Commissioner Dalman retires out in February next year. This is a powerful constitutional position which has a fixed term of 7 years ending 4 years after Erap's constitutional term ends in 2004. Dodo Mandanas will be in a position to protect Erap's ass, and defend all the skullduggery of Erap's officials, as well as hold a sword of Damocles over officials of Gloria's administration to the year 2008. Cremades is slavering over the increased contributions into the Black Hole of the Opus Dei.

If the Impeachment Trial of President Estrada might result in conviction, Father Jose Cremades' ace-in-the-hole will be Tatad's changing of his vote as the price for Gloria Macapagal's appointment of Dodo Mandanas as the next Chief of the Commission on Audit. And Pancho Villaraza as the next Secretary of Justice? Neat?

Opus Dei manned the organizations of Kokoy and Imelda during Martial Law. Opus Dei had a lock on Cory's economic program with Jesus Estanislao, Jose Cuisia and Cayetano Pedaranga. During Ramos time, Opus Dei had Movie Censor Etta Mendez to guard our morals and NTC Commissioner

Simeon Kintanar to control the disposition of media frequencies. With Erap and Gloria, Opus Dei Lord and Master, Caudillo Father Jose Cremades is aiming for the stars.

Opus Dei Dodo Mandanas may be COA head till 2008.

Opus Dei Numerary Hermilando "Dodo" Mandanas, Number three in the totem pole after Bernie Villegas and Jesus Estanislao is a strong candidate for appointment as Chairman, Commission of Audit, upon the retirement of the present COA head. He is being recommended by Raul de Guzman, whose wife and two daughters are Opus Dei, and who is the brother-in-law of President Erap Estrada. I must reveal my reservations about his pending appointment:

First of all, I must emphasize that the Office of the Commission on Audit carries with it the awesome power to exercise influence over the heads of all government agencies and departments that will have an incalculable impact on the 2001 and 2004. With a 7-year term that exceeds that of President Erap Estrada by 4 years, to the year 2008, we ask who will be safe from the machinations of the Opus Dei, intent on its pursuit of wealth and power???

Second, I sincerely doubt the loyalty of Dodo Mandanas to anyone except the Spanish overlords of Opus Dei, specifically the mysterious Father Jose Cremades. He is a highly situated member of Opus Dei, no less a numerary with vows of chastity, poverty and obedience. According Esteban Latorre, formerly an Opus Dei priest number 6 in the totem pole, he heard Father Cremades loudly complain about his affluent lifestyle, and his frequent disobedience to the rules of the Opus Dei in his role as a numerary. Yet his basic loyalty is to the Opus Dei, and it is expected that notwithstanding his shortfalls and deficiencies, he will be fully supported by Senator Kit Tatad (one of the most influential Supernumerary members of the Opus Dei) and the world-wide Opus Dei as an instrument by which their influence may be extended. The entire Philippine banking community is dominated by an Opus Dei faction which tries to control it Mafia-style, headed by former ex-CB Governor Cuisa, ex-Cory finance man Jess Estanislao (no. 2 in the Opus totem pole), and ex-World Bank employee Cidito Mapa. There are too many Opus Dei who could apply tremendous pressure to get Mandanas appointed COA head.

But just imagine what will happen when secure in his seven-year tenure as COA head, he is called upon to evaluate "anomalies" concocted by our politicians against each other. In such a case he will surely consult Father Jose Cremades and his spiritual advisers in the Opus Dei, as well as Kit Tatad, Bernardo Villegas and Jesus Estanislao, and that may lead to disaster. One must remember that while Opus Dei Mario Camacho, Lito Sandejas, Rex Drilon and Tony Ozaeta were serving Kokoy Romualdez, and while Dodo Mandanas was serving Imelda Marcos, Bernie Villegas was savagely attacking the crooked administration of President Ferdinand Marcos. Mr. Latorre who was living in the same Opus house with Bernie Villegas in the 1980s, testifies that Bernie had secret breakfast meetings with US Ambassador Bosworth at least once a week. Later, Joey Cuisia and Jesus Estanislao served Cory upon recommendation of Bernie Villegas and the late Jaime Ongpin. Such divided loyalties happen within the Opus Dei notwithstanding the vows of absolute obedience pledged to their spiritual directors. Latorre says that such divided loyalties are encouraged by Father Jose Cremades for the purpose of advancing the interest of Opus Dei in all possible areas of influence.

As COA head, Opus Dei Mandanas is a threat to all of us.

Next, I sincerely doubt Dodo Mandanas' (as COA head) commitment to public service. He has been a close associate of very controversial politicians and businessmen of doubtful reputation. He was Deputy Minister of the Human Settlements, the right-hand man to Imelda Marcos and privy to her criminal activities. He was the head of Tan Yu's Fuga Island Development Group which collapsed. He was with James Go of the Orient Bank which also collapsed. He was investment banker in Teng Puyat's Manila Bank which also collapsed. He was president of G-Tech Phils., which submitted bids for the lotto business (which the Catholic Church condemned) but his bid was rejected when his mother firm G-Tech in the USA was found to have Mafia connections, with a reputation of bribing officials in the States (a senator was actually convicted of having been bribed). He also approached Lenny de Jesus of the PMT with proposal for another gambling venture "On Line Kino."

Lastly, I sincerely think that Mandanas has his own private agenda apart from that of serving Erap Estrada or Gloria Macapagal Arroyo. According to Latorre, he violated his vows of poverty by accepting a lot of money and not turning them over to Opus Dei as a numerary should. He set up the Southern Batangas Youth Foundation to fund his campaign for governor, bought the posh Alpha Hotel in Batangas City as his political base, campaigned flying high in James Go's helicopter, and got himself elected as Batangas governor. If we cannot be sure of his loyalty to the Opus Dei, how can be sure of his loyalty to the President and to the country??

Hermilando "Dodo" Mandanas is an entrepreneur, an accountant (once worked in Carlos J. Valdez Accounting firm), management consultant and college professor (in La Salle University). He was recruited as a celibate numerary into the Opus Dei by Bernie Villegas (the first Filipino to join the Opus Dei, in Boston) and Jesus Estanislao (the first Filipino to join the Opus in the Philippines), and was considered Number 3 in the Opus Dei hierarchy when he became the right-hand man of Imelda Marcos. As number 6 in seniority and a personal assistant to Opus founder Josemaria Escriva de Balaguer up to the day he died, ex-Opus Dei priest Luis Esteban Latorre personally heard Father Jose Cremades, Spanish head of the local Opus Dei complain loudly of Dodo Mandanas' irrepressible ambitions, his affluent lifestyle, his independence and disobedience to Opus Dei rules, contained in several volumes in Latin and Spanish called "Praxis."

Having Opus Dei Mario Camacho, Rex Drilon, Tony Ozaeta and Lito Sandejas help build Kokoy's nefarious empire was bad enough. Having Opus Dei Etta Mendez as movie and TV Censor act as guardian of our morals, and Opus Dei Sim Kintanar as NTC Commissioner allocating frequencies to our media, during the Ramos Administration, was bad enough. We will regret even more having Opus Dei Dodo Mandanas as COA head, passing judgment on the actuations of our government officials in behalf of the secretive Opus Dei.

December 13-15, 2000

Part 8. Misallocation of the world's scarce resources (written for Cong. Gloria Arroyo)

Someday an alien philosopher-scientist, surveying the dying civilization of man on our planet earth, would point to a turning point in our history where we took a wrong turn that led to the demise of our race, not with a bang but with a whimper.

He would point to an increasing world population of old and dying people, dependent on a decreasing minority of young people to keep them alive and well, their churches empty, the remnants of their glorious past decaying to dust – an irreversible situation that came about when the leaders of advanced nations decided on the policy of zero population growth to conserve the world's scarce resources, and supplying the less developed nations with the means to comply with it.

This policy simply was to change the mindset of mankind for the instant gratification of the sex-drive by means of contraceptives and permissiveness, instead of self-discipline and responsible parenthood. The result was the proliferation of divorce and separations, single parenthood and the break-up of the family as the basic nucleus of society in advanced societies, while doing very little to limit the population of the poor, the unskilled and the uneducated.

I am an economist, concerned with the allocation of the world's scarce resources for the unlimited needs and wants of mankind. It bothers me to think of the sheer waste of food in advanced nations, thrown away in the trash cans of homes and restaurants, of surplus crops buried in the mountains to maintain high price levels, of inappropriate diets that lead of epidemics of obesity – enough to feed all the starving people of the world, if distributed with generosity and efficiency.

It bothers me to think of the amount of the world's resources being spent in manufacturing weapons of mass destruction, in developing military capacity to destroy our cities and infrastructures, and being used to kill and maim innocent women and children.

It bothers me to think of all the world resources devoted to the pollution of the environment and the dangers of climate change.

You want to protect our people from AIDS and HIV? Isn't it cheaper and better to discourage irresponsible and deviant sex?

Isn't a lot cheaper to concentrate our resources in developing such medicines that have in past rendered extinct such plagues as the bubonic, the smallpox, typhoid, cholera, the deadly strain of influenza, and in the future AIDS and HIV?

Because we are misallocating our resources for measures that will someday lead to the demise of civilization as we know it, a future of old people dying, dependent on an ever shrinking youthful workforce – and because I am above all an economist, I am voting against the RH bill, in the hope, however dim, that mankind will allocate its scarce resources to nuclear disarmament, to clean energy, to the generous and efficient redistribution of food to poor nations, and to the ideals of truth, beauty and goodness.

Part 9. Raul Manglapus never banned fiestas!

IN the last part of June 1991, Senator Heherson "Sonny" Alvarez, Chairman of the committee on natural resources and ecology, proposed that experts study the possibility of strategic bombing of selected spots around Mt. Pinatubo to divert mudflows from populated areas.

And everyone snickered. Derision in the press consigned Alvarez's Pinatubo bombing to such nincompoopery as Congressman Vera's outlawing of typhoons, President Ramon Magsaysay's abrogation of the law of supply and demand, and Raul Manglapus' abolition of fiestas.

Hehehe Alvarez can take satisfaction from the fact that such strategic bombing was used successfuly in the 1935 eruption of Mauna Loa in Hawaii, but he cannot escape the derision of the press.

Vera's bill was a perfectly valid proposal to study the typhoon with the view of diverting it or dissipating its force. Today it is possible to seed hurricanes, even bomb the storm's eye to divert and dissipate it. Up to now, long after he's been dead, Vera is still known to have attempted to abolish typhoons.

Ramon Magsaysay's remark about abrogating the law of supply and demand is a complete fabrication, a politician's joke to show up Monching's lack of sophistication. But the joke acquired a life of its own and will probably last forever.

Manglapus' proposal regarding fiestas, sought not to abolish it but to utilize it for capital formation and productive endeavor, like pig raising, duck raising, credit unions, scholarship funding -- instead of conspicuous consumption and give-away hospitality. A perfectly valid movement which I headed as president of *Fiestas for Progress*, was practically laughed out of existence.

My friend Raul Manglapus screams with pain every time he sees reprinted for the nth time the canard that as a senator he introduced a bill to abolish fiestas. Max Soliven in 1987 wrote that Raul "proposed a law banning fiestas" and that he was "jeered and booted out of the Senate in the 1967 elections." And now Teddy Benigno does the same thing in his Star column dated March 21, 1997, writing that Manglapus "got off a Senate bill to ban fiestas and was bopped bowlegged by a fiesta loving citizenry and Congress." Well, Max and Teddy, pardon me for living but I was there as the president of *Fiestas for Progress*, and I know that:

(1) Raul never filed a bill banning fiestas. We proposed not to ban the fiesta but to use it for productive purposes, such as saving capital for projects like *balut* and salted eggs in Pateros, where our experiment became successful. No need for a law.

(2) Raul did not lose an election to the senate simply because he did not run for the senate in 1967. I did, along with Ninoy Aquino, Soc Rodrigo, Camilo Osias, and Maria KK the Censor; only Ninoy won. Nobody could have jeered Manglapus then, nor booted him out in an election he did not participate in.

(3) The next time Raul Maglapus did run was his third party (Progressive) bid for the presidency in 1965, and he and Macapagal lost to Ferdinand Marcos. He then ran in 1970 for the Constitutional Convention. He won in the first district of Rizal with the highest number of votes in the entire country.

Fiestas For Progress was a worthwhile project

Raul Manglapus was my school-boy hero, the champion orator and composer of the Ateneo's signature song, "Blue Eagle." He was at the time senator of the republic, and aspiring candidate for the presidency of our land. I was at the time the president of the Philippine Chamber of Industries, and soon to be appointed to the presidential cabinet of President Diosdado Macapagal as Chairman of the National Economic Council and Presidential Administrator of Community Development (PACD).

Senator Raul Manglapus and I organized the "Fiestas for Progress" movement, of which I was President and he was

Chairman and moving spirit. Economist Augusto Cesar Espiritu, later Ambassador to West Germany, was with us as vice president. Jesus Tanchanco, soon to be NFA Aministrator, was treasurer; and Jorge Lorredo as PRO. Also Arturo "Bong" Tangco later to be Minister of Agriculture and indefatigable loverboy. Raul was chairman.

Mrs. J.B., widow of Col. Arsenio de Borja, who headed the movement in Pateros, sent me a pamphlet we issued for Fiestas for Progress, which set up pilot projects with four basic objectives:

o To cut down on excessive expenditures on food and drink on the fiesta, to minimize games of chance and contests like dancing and beauty pageants, and give more importance to contests for the best pig, chicken, cow, and the biggest vegetables grown, highest yielding land use, and other useful pursuits.

o To use fund-raising activities like lotteries and cockfights, reserving part of the winnings to accumulate capital for Credit Unions and Cooperatives.

o To minimize borrowings for the fiesta celebration, minimize extravagant expenses like opening one's doors indiscriminately to strangers, many of who flit from one fiesta to another cadging free food and drinks. It is better to entice out-of-towners with special events like the floating flower festival, Hala Bira, and church festivities, and ask them to pay for their own food and shelter, as we ask foreigners who come to our shores.

o To prove to the nation that investments, increased incomes and economic progress are possible if there is cooperation and willingness to change.

The bottom line is that fiestas should bring more money into the town instead of out of the town; and such money should be used to create opportunities for economic advancement. Unfortunately, the word spread that we were abolishing the fiesta, and we became the subject of jokes and laughed at behind our backs.

The Pateros experiment showed that the people served less food and drinks in their homes during fiesta, holding family reunions without going into debt. Money came into Pateros as visitors patronized stores and vendors. And the people were able to set up with their savings one of the biggest credit unions in the country, through which they sent their children to school, revived their faltering industries and set up new ones, and freed themselves from the clutches of loan sharks.

Getting a US "spy" to eat balut

We had a lot of fun, Raul Manglapus and the rest of us, pursuing the objectives of *Fiestas For Progress*. We descended into town fiestas determined to do some good, We were welcomed into homes, into churches, even into cockpits where we found ourselves watching this barbaric sport, and comparing it with the bullfighting of Spain. We were given permission to speak in the cockpit, they did not even bother to boo us, they just ignored our presence amidst the babble of betting. We came out with the conviction that cockfighting is ingrained in the Filipino soul, its gambling practices etched in his character, and nothing short of an atom bomb can put them asunder

Our most amusing experience concerned John Esterline of the USIS propaganda agency, about whom so many unkind things were written and said. He wanted to maneuver the Philippine American Cultural Foundation into an outright American propaganda agency. The Americans contributed $1 million, at the time worth only P4 million, while asking for a Philippine contribution of P14 million in cash and land plus continuing tax exemption. At the same time the Americans made it clear that they will run the whole show. Ridiculous.

Esterline was also pilloried for perpetrating the "bomb hoax" that accused Filipinos of trying to bomb an American school house full of children -- an incident that triggered a series of demonstrations against the US Embassy. Editorial writer Adrian Cristobal wrote a series of editorials on the bomb hoax that won him the year's prestigious Esso Award (later abolished).

After receiving the award, Adrian was promptly fired from the Evening News at the instigation of Esterline, whom they accused of being a CIA agent spying on and subverting a friendly people.

If Esterline was a spy, he was not a successful one, and maybe that is why he is so likeable. The only time he was able to advance the interest of America was during the Pateros Fiesta when he tagged along with Raul Manglapus and myself in one of our *Fiestas for Progress* sorties.

"Hey, Esterline, know what is the greatest riddle of all time? It is this: Which comes first, the chicken or the egg? Well now, you see before you the answer to that riddle, a *balut*. My friend, you eat a balut and you acquire the wisdom of the ages, for the *balut* is both the chicken and the egg. Care to try?"

This is the acid test Filipinos should apply to their American friends. Only one out of a thousand Americans would try. And 99 out of a hundred who try, would get laid up for a week, absolutely sick.

But our friend Esterline nonchalantly ate five baluts -- soup, chicken, yolk, white hard core and all -- smacked his lips and asked for more! In shocked desperation, we handed him a pack of cheap, smelly, black, bittersweet *Pagkakaisa cigarillos*. He did not smoke them, he ate them too!

Later Esterline turned the table on us. He picked out a US marine, trained him for the *balut*-eating contest in Pateros, and watched with a toothy grin, as the marine won the contest hands down, swallowing 18 baluts in 5 minutes, face smeared, mouth drooling, nose dripping with what-not -- while the Filipinos in the audience turned pale-green and hectic blue, absolutely sick with nausea.

April 3-7, 1997, ISYU

Part 10. The Sunrise Mass for God's Troubador

Would I might wake/ St. Francis in you all/ Brother of birds and trees,/ GOD's TROUBADOUR! –Vachel Lindsay

Every year since 1992, in October, the month of the Feast Day of St. Francis Of Assisi, my late sister-in-law Ditas Lichauco helped organize a Sunrise Mass at 4 or 5 o'clock in the morning in our Dasmariñas Village. It is a special mass dedicated to the preservation of the environment, Mother Nature and all living things – ecological awareness through the venue of worship, to whom St. Francis dedicated most of his life. Ditas died late last year. This year is the first time Ditas is not around to take charge of the Sunrise Mass, so my other sister-in-law Luisa, now known as a Maryknoll nun, Sister Marissa, continues the tradition. This year, the Sunrise Mass, celebrated last Saturday, October 21, offered the gift of Peace, of Hope, of Love, of the Millennium as the start of a new day. To our fellow Filipinos and fellow men all over the world:

We offer the Gift Of Peace, peace among ourselves and with all nations. Not just the absence of war, but the presence of peace based on tolerance, understanding, mutual respect, a healthy relationship between all people, the peace and goodwill that bridges the gap between races, between cultures, between genders, between religions, between the old and the young, between the rich and the poor, between the straight and the gay. We offer the gift of peace to the Moslems and Jews of the Middle East, the Moslems and Christians of Bosnia, the Hindus and Moslems of Kashmir, Tamil Hindus and Sinhalese Buddhists of Sri Lanka, the Catholics and Protestants of Northern Ireland, and very very especially to our brother Moslems and Christians in Mindanao.

We offer the gift of hope. For we who would transform a nation, we who would renovate a stagnant society, we cannot do so by driving our people to despair, or infecting them with hatred, distrust of one another, self-doubt, and colonial double allegiance. We must like the prophets of old, kindle and fan an extravagant hope, based on faith in ourselves and in our God if we are to inspire our people to constructive action.

We offer the gift of Love, not only Eros, the love of a man and a woman for each other that actuates the instinct to preserve the human race, but also fraternal love, the love and loyalty of brothers, sisters. parents and relatives for each other. Also the love of country, nation and people, a sense of nationhood, a sense of belonging to each other, a sense of common destiny. Not only Eros, fraternal love, love of country, but also the love of God who is the Father and Creator of us all. And above all is Agape, the love that knows no bounds, for all living things and for all of God's Creation.

We offer the gift of the Millennium, a break in the continuum, a pause in timeless eternity, to reassess the past and plan for the future, to appreciate what has happened before and to renew our faith in next one thousand years, to acknowledge our mistakes and to begin anew, all over again, and bring peace, hope and love to the people of today and tomorrow, and above all to take better care of the planet Earth that is our common home.

We offer all these to God and to ourselves in this sunrise mass of our new day of our next millennium. Amen.

October 23, 2000, The Philippine Post

Part 11. Ateneo, La Salle, UST, Letran

1. Collegialas go to La Salle, Ateneo to find husbands, to UP for an ideology

I resist the temptation of contributing a short item in the Capus Alaskahan series, involving jokes about Ateneo and make instead a longish article for which I expect to be paid. *Pangalatoks* are more *kuripot* than Ilocanos, you know.

I asked my son Atom what are the differences between the schools he and his friends attended. He said:

In La Salle, the Christian Brothers push you to the wall, saying "You're no good. You're no good. Dammit, fight back, it's a jungle world out there!"

Ateneo, on the other hand, is not the jungle world La Salle is, it is the Kingdom of Heaven. The Jesuits never say "You're no good," they say, "You're good, you're the best. Go out and conquer the world, we're right behind you!"

The University of the Philippines is neither a jungle world nor the kingdom of heaven, it is the world as it is. In UP the professors never say, "You're no good." They never say "You're the best." They just do not give a good goddam.

After a few years of hearing that crap about being the best, the Atenean begins to believe it of himself, he becomes super-*mayabang* like myself and my editor Danny Mariano.

You can always tell an Atenean as far as a block away, he struts around as if he has an apple under each of his armpits. He is smug, self assured and arrogant. He is a talkative know-it all. He writes the most beautiful love letters. And he never suffers defeat, his Ateneo spirit dictates that every setback is a "moral victory." When an Atenean says to an acquaintance, "So you're an Atenean!" the unspoken message is "Wow, you must be as good as I am."

The La Sallites are always on the defensive and on the offensive, that is why they are good in business. But there is no such thing as a La Salle spirit, nothing that binds students together as La Sallites. They are forever divided along three ethnic lines, and they are not even on speaking terms with one another. There are the mestizos, who glory in their whiteness, good looks and sex prowess, who invariably get a job at the San Miguel Corporation, or migrate and join the white trash of

Australia. There are the Chinese who own the country, rich, clannish, marrying only within their own circles, closely guarded and forever wary of being kidnapped. Then there are the Pinoys who are left to fend themselves, with a little sense of self-worth, many of them either follow Bernie Villegas into the Opus Dei to rub shoulders with God and the wealthy, or go to Ateneo to acquire self-confidence and insolence.

There is no collective term for UP students. There are only the fractious fraternities constantly at war with each other, and taking the role of a welfare system that takes care of the stupid and the indigent. But most are very bright, the best of every barangay in the archipelago, together with Ateneans and La Sallites seeking a real genuine education. And they would really get a good education if only the UP professors can be depended upon to attend their classes regularly.

Those pretty girls from the exclusive colleges, where do they go? They go to La Salle and Ateneo to find husbands, they go to UP for a cause and an ideology.

2. Ateneo, Harvard -- excellence, old money and old boy network

My son Atom (A for Alfredo, Tom for Tomas, Atom Bum we call him), a graduate of La Salle and Ateneo decided to get his MBA, he took the GMAT tests given by the US Embassy with flying colors. I advised him to apply to entrance to Stanford, MIT and Harvard, rated in that order the best business schools at the time. To my surprise, he answered, "I am applying only to Harvard Business School. It's Harvard or none at all."

Stanford was rated the best with its group dynamics approach, MIT's Sloan Institute the next best with its "mathematical models." Harvard was third with its case studies approach, and it was the most expensive, costing about P1 million a year. "Explain yourself, young man," I told the Atomic Bum. He said:

School ratings depend on the votes of business executives, graduate students and school professors, and the ratings on the best schools change every year. But every time a list surfaces, the others may come and go but Harvard is always among the best. "I go to Harvard to it is the one closest to being like Ateneo. It has a long history. Harvard men send their sons and grandsons to Harvard, as Ateneans do theirs.

There is a sense of belonging among Ateneans and Harvard men that transcends generations, that closes the gap between the old and the young, and binds classmates forever -- an old boy network. Harvard and Ateneo have been in existence so long that they are inhabited by old money, financial wizards and high IQ. Rich classmates even organize companies to accommodate classmates who need a job.

Me, the only MIT graduates I am close to are those who graduated with me. When Atom graduated from Harvard, the chairman of First National Bank of Chicago, who is a Harvard graduate of another generation, sent his jet to bring my son Atom from Boston to Chicago, interviewed him personally and hired him on the spot. That is how strong the old boy network is -- I know of no Atenean or a Harvard man who ever permanently out of a job. There are other schoolmates who own companies or are influential inside others, who can give him a job. Atom got a job when all his friends from Wharton, Columbia, and MIT were jobless at the time of the Great Recession in the USA.

The same advantages hold true for Ateneans. They belong to an old boy network that is based on comradeship, inherited wealth, a tradition of excellence, brilliance of mind combined with athletic prowess, and a common heritage of role models - Jose Rizal, Claro M. Recto, Ninoy Aquino, Raul Manglapus, Manny Pelaez, President Eddie Ramos (an Ateneo MBA graduate), Vice-President Erap Estrada (thrown out of high school for fighting an American classmate named Wilson).

No La Sallite ever emerged to run the country, but La Salle did give us two of our greatest nationalists -- Lorenzo Tañada and Jose W. Diokno.

We cannot trust UP to run the country. From UP came President Manuel Roxas who gave the Americans parity rights, and President Ferdinand Marcos who gave us Martial Law and the dark ages.

3. Spanish Dominicans evolved like bedbugs and cockroaches

Now let's write of Letran, reputedly the depository of those not admitted into or thrown out of Ateneo and La Salle. Actually

Letran is the oldest of all our schools having been started in 1587 by Father Pedro Bolaños OP, merged with Sto. Domingo Church in 1611, and took the name of Colegio de Niños de San Juan de Letran in 1620. It is therefore older than Santo Tomas (1611), older than Harvard (1636), and much older than Ateneo (1859).

Letran produced some of our outstanding contemporaries: Cesar Zalamea, Ric Manrique, Fred Luarca, Herminio Astorga, Johnny Ibazeta, Louie Tabuena, Freddie Webb, Jack Rodriguez, Vice President Fernando Lopez, Peping Cojuangco and if you Ateneans don't stop laughing derisively, I will add that the Dominicans who run Letran and Santo Tomas also gave us five presidents: Aguinaldo, Quezon, Laurel, Osmeña, and Macapagal. Ateneo and La Salle never gave us a single president. The nearest the Jesuits got to the presidency is teaching Magsaysay how to deliver a speech.

Letran also produced more revolutionaries than all the schools combined: Apolinario Mabini, Emilio Jacinto, Marcelo del Pilar, Padre Jose Burgos, Padre Jacinto Zamora, Artemio "Vibora" Ricarte, Dr. Jose Panganiban, Jose Torres Bugallon, Enrique Mendiola, Gregorio Aglipay, Jose Rizal, Emilio Aguinaldo, Manuel Quezon, my own grandfather, Daniel Maramba.

I pointed this out to my grandfather, a veteran of the revolution, who became an assemblyman and senator. He explained: "Letran and Sto. Tomas bred so many revolutionaries, because we students found our Dominican teachers so hateful, we could not wait to revolt against Spain." My grandfather was a good Catholic until he met the Dominican friars, whereupon he became a 33rd degree Free Mason. So did Jose Rizal and the rest of our heroes whose 1898 revolution was really directed against the Spanish friars, especially the Dominicans.

Jose Rizal in his El Filibusterismo wrote scathingly of them, in terms of Father Millón who would insult, degrade, and inflict his ignorance on Placido Penitente and the 234 students in his class, in the words of Rizal, "to be brutalized, to have their dignity outraged and their youthful enthusiasms turned to indolence and hatred," and called upon God to "demand a strict accounting of those responsible for minds darkened and blinded, for the outraged human dignity, for the wasted years and fruitless labor," brought about by such teachers.

I thought Spanish Dominicans were already extinct, like the dodo bird and the dinosaurs. But they are still here, alive, without any missing parts and still in working condition, hardly evolving from their original form, like the cockroach and the bedbug, as anti-Filipino as ever. Their professors (Molina, Zaide, etc.) wrote books glorifying Spanish colonization, including an offensive chapter, "Did Rizal like Mestizos?" in which Rizal with tongue-in-cheek wrote that mestizos are superior to Indios. They forged the religious retraction of Rizal. They vigorously the Noli-Fili bill sponsored by Recto whom they called a Communist. They resisted the Filipinization of Sto. Tomas. And they foisted on us a Filipino saint who is nothing but a Dominican lackey and a congenital coward.

October 3-7, 1996, ISYU

Part 12. Insurance firms are cheating you

After World War II a group of Jewish American entrepreneurs from Shanghai came to the Philippines and set up the Philippine American Life Insurance Company.

It had the knack of bringing very influential people into its organization, among them Paul V. McNutt, American Governor General; Ramon V. del Rosario, then president of Jaycee International; Leonides Virata, a member of Marcos's cabinet; Cesar Zalamea, closely connected with Marcos; Jose Cuisia, Cory's Central Bank Governor. It had the knack of getting concessions from the government, like the precious land on United Nations Avenue in exchange for some nondescript property. Till recently, it always managed to have very, very, very, very friendly relations with every Insurance Commissioners appointed, in the same way the three oil companies influenced any government official in charge of energy. Thus insured, Phil-Am Life proceeded to dominate over 90 percent, so it is estimated, of the life insurance business. It still is the biggest insurance company in the Philippines, with CAP Life Insurance a close second.

Of course, at the outset of my career, I had myself insured by Philippine American Life. I was talked into buying a 20-year Pay Life Insurance Plan, on which I paid regular premiums, part of which had "cash value" that may be borrowed or encashed any

time. This constituted the savings feature of the insurance plan.
Also, I got a college endowment plan for my eldest son, Ronnie.

I cancelled all Phil-Am insurance plans years later when I
found out that:

*The Phil-Am Life used my savings (cash value) to buy
assets that appreciated 25 percent a year, while paying me a
measly six percent per annum. I could have done better putting
my money in a time deposit or in blue chip stocks.

* The face value, the insurance part of the plan, was
constantly eroded by high inflation, so that what is supposed to
give my family full security after my death, will upon my death
provide only enough to pay for my funeral expenses.

* One of the insurance plans involved a face value to be
paid in dollars upon my death. The Phil-Am Life repudiated this
dollar obligation upon the decontrol of our economy in 1961,
saying that when I die, my heirs will be paid in peso at the rate of
P2 to $1 as the exchange value was during the previous Import
Control period.

* Most important of all, I found out that I was paying a lot
more money in premiums than foreign companies were charging
abroad for the same insurance plan. The Phil-Am Life could
overcharge us Filipinos because it had an almost complete
monopoly of life insurance in the Philippines.

* Another was an Educational Endowment plan bought by
my mother for her eldest grandson, Ronnie. We paid good money
for the premiums, but when the plan matured, what was supposed
to be enough to pay for an entire college education in Ateneo was
not even enough to pay for one semester.

The only way I could have had any winning advantage over
the Phil-Am was to die within five years after I took out the
insurance. But apparently, I lived too long and I feel that I was
cheated. I was screwed front, back and center.

A perverse bet

Life, in modern times, moves very much in the fast lane and
is so uncertain, so unpredictable, so full of unexpected dangers
that insurance has become an absolute necessity.

For security and peace of mind, modern man needs to
insure and protect himself and his loved ones against the risks of
sudden death, unforeseen medical expenses, unemployment, fire

and other disasters. Without such insurance, one risks unexpected bankruptcy and penury.

When you pay an insurance premium, you are essentially making a bet with the insurance company. Perversely you bet that a great misfortune will be fall you within a specified period of time. The insurance company bets that the law of averages mathematically computed, will find you in good fortune during that period. Payments to beneficiaries are in the nature of consuelo de bobo.

If disaster strikes, you win the bet and the company compensates you for your loss. If nothing happens, you lose the bet and all your premiums are forfeited. Thousands upon thousands of people contribute premium payments to very few companies. Thus the payments are gathered in a pool of funds that serves to guarantee that the risks are averaged out among many and the losses of the few unfortunates are adequately compensated for.

Insurance contributes to the economy by providing for the replacement for property lost or destroyed and for sustaining finances affected by illness, injury or death. And it contributes further to the economy in another way. The huge reserves accumulated by insurers provide industry with funds for capital expansion or other investments. To protect the interests of the public in general, the government regulates insurance companies through the Insurance Commission with three objectives, namely, to require insurers to maintain their financial soundness, to provide the policyholders with the maximum protection and fairness of treatment and to make sure company officers, agents, brokers and adjusters are trustworthy.

There is a catch. The risk to be insured against must be "contingent," that is, events must occur without the control of the insured or the insurer, subject only to the law of averages. In addition, you, the insured, must have an "insurable interest" so that even when you win the bet, you share part of the loss. A policy without such an insurable interest is deemed to be a gambling contract and therefore void, such as when you insure the house of a stranger against fire. The principal types of insurance are: Annuity, Fire Insurance, Health Insurance, Liability Insurance, Life Insurance, Workers' Compensation. In addition, the government provides a system of social security, Medicare,

Bank Deposit Insurance against bank failure, even insurance against crop failures.

The insurer amasses small contributions from many persons exposed to risks to create a fund that is used to reimburse those insured who actually suffer loss. These contributions are called premiums. A contract of insurance is called a policy. There are many kinds of life insurance plans, but only one can be said to be a good risk proposition, the "term insurance," a strong unadulterated bet common to all insurers. All other plans, including the so-called Pay Life, incorporate "savings features" that add all sorts of unseen costs for the insured.

Term Insurance

There are many types of insurance: Term, Pay Life and as many variations as there are insurance companies.

Term Insurance is the backbone of the industry, the premiums paid per year for every hundred thousands pesos insurance mathematically computed by actuarians on the basis of census statistics, average life expectancies and records of previous persons insured.

Then there are the various Pay Life insurance plans. A 20-year Pay Life for instance requires the insured to pay premiums in equal installments only for 20 years. But the face value is paid to the beneficiaries only at the time of death. The Pay Life plan incorporates a savings feature that accumulates a "cash value" which one may encash at any time, or borrow at nominal interest. If the insured could not keep up with the payments, he may use the accumulated cash values to pay the premiums. When the cash values dip to zero and no payments are forthcoming, the insurance is considered lapsed and the insured gets nothing for all the premiums paid in previous years.

The 30-year Pay Life, of course, requires payment of premiums in equal installments for 30 years. The Whole Life plan requires payments throughout one's whole lifetime. In the Participating Life Plan, the premiums payment are invested by the company and the insured participates in the profits after insurance payments to the insured incurring losses are paid. The trouble with these life insurance plans with savings features is that insurance companies give very little returns on the insured's savings and investment. The returns are far smaller than what is given by banks, investment houses and even blue chip investment in stock exchanges. And what is not usually known is that the premium payments, especially in the first years and in progressively decreasing amounts throughout the period of insurance, go into the pockets of the insurance agents as commissions. Thus insurance experts like Dr. Peter Sen, consultant of the Insurance Commission, tell us that insurance firms are bad investment houses and do not recommend life insurance to those who want to save. Sen adds that taxes on insurance in the Philippines is one of the highest in the world, that in these days of open economy where ASEAN nations are welcome to compete in each other's countries, our five percent tax and documentary taxes make our companies uncompetitive against Thai firms.

For maximum protection in life insurance, avoid the ones with savings feature that give you too little returns with most of what you pay going to the insurance agents. The best and cheapest is a straight bet, a Term Insurance, renewable ever so often. Increase your insurance in consonance with your income and the rate of inflation. Pay Life is good if you die within five years; if you live longer, it will pay your heirs only enough to pay for your funeral expenses. Avoid endowment plans. I bought one to insure the college education of my son. After 20 years, it was not even enough to pay one semester. Go for the CAP college assurance plan, which pays future tuition in full exchange of present payments equal to today's prices, plus reimbursement of all payments 10 years after graduation – a hedge against inevitable devaluation and inflation and a damn good deal.

Other non-life insurance policies

There are other forms of non-life insurance. The Health Maintenance Organizations (HMO) or Home Care, Blue Cross, Health Shield and Maxicare, provide insurance against sudden and unaffordable medical expenses.

The SSS (for private workers) and the GSIS (for government workers) provide social security to its members than run the gamut from life insurance to unemployment compensation, medicare and death benefits. The Philippine National Health Corporation provides both Social Assistance and Social Insurance, a boon to poor, a bane for the rich member.

But the most important is the Property Insurance which insures against property loss at sea, against fire, flood and other disasters on buildings, equipment, inventory and other productive assets. Also against car accidents and third party liability. No actuarial expertise is needed and insurance rates vary from year to year. Insurance firms spread and share the risk by reinsurance with other companies abroad. There is also Risk Selection by a unique firm, Lloyds of London, which will insure: a singer's voice, a pianist's hands, or any part of anatomy; also items of art.

There are three characters involved between the insured and the insurance company: the insurance agent who represent the company, the insurance broker who represent the insured and the insurance adjuster who stands between the settles conflicting claims of both. The adjuster decides whether a claim should be paid or not and how much should be paid.

The most important to the insured is the insurance broker who calls attention to the three pitfalls of property insurance: over insurance, under insurance and the hidden mysteries of fine print. In property insurance, the base line is the replacement value of the property insured. If it is insured above this value, it is considered over-insured and in case of loss, the company pays only the replacement value of the property. If it is insured the value, it is considered under-insured and the insured is considered co-insurer for the difference so in case of loss, the company pays only the portion of the replacement value that it is supposed to insure.

Examples. If the property has a replacement value of P1 million and you insure it for P2 million, when it is completely burned down, you are paid only P1 million. You have lost the extra premiums you paid for the over-evaluation. On the other hand, if you insure it for only P750,000 and it is totally lost, the company considers that it is insured only for three-fourths of its value and you will be paid only P750,000. If it is not totally lost, even if there are few posts left, those are deducted from the replacement value and proportionately deducted from the compensation payment. You get screwed both ways. That is why you need an insurance broker to advise you. This broker represents you but his services are free; the company pays him a commission just like the insurance agent. Likewise, the company pays the insurance adjuster who arbitrates the claims of both the insurer and the insured.

Fine Print and Car Insurance
There is a lot of fine print in the insurance policy that prejudices the interest of the insured.

The insurance broker calls attention to these in representation of the insured. And if need be, he re-negotiates amendments embodied in a supplemental agreement. Remember this well: The supplemental agreement supercedes the fine print and any insurance company who says otherwise is cheating you.

What are the risk embodied in the fine print that can be fixed by a supplemental agreement? One is the coverage of valuable items in the house, like paintings by Vicente Manansala and Fernando Amorsolo, each of which may be worth more than P10 million. Our sculptures by Solomon Saprid, worth may be a million because he is still alive. All these items, if lost, will be compensated for in amount of P200 each as per fine print, unless covered by a supplemental agreement, inventorying each, giving its evaluation by competent authority, complete with pictures. Also, when a car is stolen, according to the fine print, the insurance company buys you a new car 10 months after the theft; unless a supplemental agreement forces the company to compensate you sooner, you may find yourself riding taxis for months on end.

In the final analysis, it is better and cheaper for you to hire an insurance broker to negotiate for you and to explain to you all the mumbo-jumbo and techno-quackery in the fine print of your insurance policy. And to advise you what insurance companies are *balasubas* and slow in paying claims. It costs you nothing. The insurance company pays his commission.

Will the insurance company pay for all the repair bills for the damaged car? No, the insured is considered a co-insurer and must pay for the first P1,000 of the repair bill, depending on the policy. Can an insured choose a repair shop for his damaged car or his he at the mercy of the insurance company when it comes to choice? He can, but the most expensive he can choose is the casa or official service center. And the company will pay only if the damaged to the car is officially reported in a police report. So get a policeman to make an official report on the accident.

Before a vehicle is registered by the Land Transportation Office (LTO), the owners are required to present a certificate of insurance coverage. What is required by the LTO is the compulsory Third Party Liability insurance, which compensates traffic victims for death and bodily injuries according to a fix schedule. This third party liability insurance does not, however, assure the car owner that he can get away from any liability for physical harm he may cause to another person or to another person's property — only the court can decide adequate compensation.

In addition to this insurance required by the LTO, the car owner may contract insurance for loss of theft, for his own bodily injury, for damaged to his own car and even for excess liability, which may amount to thousands of pesos. Also, for a No-Fault indemnity by which the company pays any claim for death or bodily injury to a third person without the necessity of providing fault or negligence of any kind under certain conditions. More tomorrow.

Insurance recommendations

Many insurance companies are fly-by-night outfits which have a habit of going into bankruptcy every time they are faced with large claims for compensation.

This happens after a big fire or earthquake. Some insurance companies, so fast in collecting premiums, have a reputation for being *tuso* and *balasubas*, delaying the payment of claims *ad nauseum*. What can you do if the insurance company gives you a problem or a difficult time? Short of going to court, you can report it to the Insurance Commissioner and/or deal with a fair insurance adjuster to resolve your claim. To avoid all this, get yourself an honest and competent insurance broker to represent you, to advise you and choose an honest insurance company to issue you an insurance policy that s fair and just.

To recapitulate what we advised in our five articles on insurance:

For your life insurance needs, a straight Term Insurance is best and cheapest. Insurance plans with a savings feature usually yield very little on savings and pay a mint in commission to the insurance agent. That is why insurance agents twist your arm to buy Pay Life insurance policies. You'd be a sucker to fall for it, unless you intend to kill yourself within five years. The company pays you very little for the use of your money. You might as well put your savings in a time deposit or money market or in the stocks.

Avoid endowment policies which pay you a fixed sum at maturity. It is a racket. You are vulnerable against devaluation and inflation. For your children's education, go to CAP for a College Assurance Plan. If you pay them the cost of education at today's prices, they guarantee they will pay for your child's education when he is of age, no matter what the tuition costs in the future. Then 10 years after graduation, they reimburse your child with all the money you have paid. It is a good deal all around, better than the lousy deal I got from Phil-Am Life, under whose endowment plan my child got a college fund that was not even enough to pay for one semester.

For property insurance, get an insurance broker to help you at no cost. Mine is Salvador Lacson who has his own under-insurance. You get thoroughly screwed both ways if you don't. And get your broker to explain the fine print in the policy and if need be, negotiate for a supplemental agreement that will supercede any fine print. Be sure your property is covered for whatever you want: war, earthquake, typhoon, flood, lightning, gas or nuclear explosion, oil spill, environmental damage, acts of God or the devil, or whatever. Pay the extra premium, if you must.

Get your insurance broker to recommend a good insurance company, with a solid reputation of financial strength and liquidity, and of competence, dependability and honesty. For life insurance, try CAP Life. They are second in resources and second to none in performance. Canada Life is also all right. Phil-Am Life has already made enough money during its long years of practical monopoly so give others a chance.

With the open market policy, a lot of new players are coming in from abroad. Shop for the best deal. Insure yourself and your loved ones against the uncertainties of our modern world. It is worth it. And good luck to you all.

August 19-26, 1997

ooooo

Chapter Nine: THE NATIONS

Part 1. Greece; Where Democracy Began

Listen, listen. That is the transition between the 3rd and 4th movement of Beethoven's Fifth Symphony – one of the most famous passages in symphonic music. Listen.

It may be fanciful and over imaginative on my part but it seems to me that these millennial years are a transitional period in human history, like the end of the 3rd movement of Beethoven's Fifth Symphony. There is this moment when the 3rd movement has ended, but the 4th movement has not begun. One waits, hushed and expectant while a sinister figure on the strings like a goblin, weaves back and forth across a slow insistent, rhythmic beat from the tympani. E. M. Forster in his novel "Howard's End" likens this particular passage to a march of goblins – evil, mischievous, misshapen sprites wandering over the universe from end to end. Forster writes:

"The music started with the goblin walking quietly over the universe from end to end. Others followed him. They observed in passing that there is no such thing as splendor or heroism in the world… It was as if the splendor of life might blow over and waste into steam and froth. In its dissolution one heard the terrible ominous note, and a goblin, with increased malignity, walked over the universe from end to end. Panic and emptiness! Panic and emptiness! Even the flaming ramparts of the world might fall."

To some unseen watcher from the skies, an interplanetary scientist and philosopher perched in his UFO and studying closely the events on planet Earth, to one who has seen great civilizations rise and fall, the new millennium must seem like the transitional passage between the 3rd and 4th movement of Beethoven's Fifth Symphony. An era has just ended. Another one has yet to begin. The high tide of Western Imperialism has ebbed; the apparent renaissance of great colonial powers with their mighty fleets and armies is but a backward glance at glories which can never return. The Communist Revolution has petered out. China, which regards itself as the heir of revolution, waxes fat like a bloated capitalist on its material progress. The United States, the leader of the colonial powers, stands alone in Iraq and Afghanistan, abandoned by its allies, alone with its puppets, caught in the quicksand of a senseless war that may never end. As a Frenchman once remarked: "The United States is the only nation in the world that has progressed from barbarism to decadence without first going through the process of being civilized." A balance of terror has gripped the world and it seems that the splendor of life has indeed boiled over and wasted to steam and froth. Panic and emptiness, panic and emptiness!

But new nations are emerging, and by the weight of their numbers they are making their presence felt in the United Nations – that universal arena when men and nations meet to weigh words, exchange esteem, assign trusts, seal bonds and chart a new era in the destiny of man.

Of all the nations, the Philippines is most unique – it is the only nation where East meets West in a perfect blending of cultures – the only English speaking country, the only Christian nation in all of Asia – we seem to be everywhere, the biggest foreign group of nurses, doctors and students in the United States and Europe, the biggest group of itinerant workers and sailors; the most scattered group of musicians in the capitals of Asia, the most boisterous tourists in the world. We are in Africa building roads, in Vietnam as engineers and doctors. And our politicians and businessman scurry to every world conference and dominate every one with their loquacity, if not their eloquence.###

As tourists, unlike the Chinese or Japanese, Filipinos never keep to themselves. There is something irritating about our perpetual curiosity. We poke around one's monuments, scrawl our names on the walls, pester one with our eternal questions and chatter all the time, and seem to be perpetually arguing and quarreling among ourselves. "Filipinos are children, how can we take them seriously?" an American once told me.

Yet that was exactly the same remark made by an Egyptian priest to a Greek named Solon, as recorded by Plato 2,500 years ago. "The Greeks are children. Clever of course, but still children," said the Egyptian priest in the year 600 before Christ. At the time the Egyptian Colossus still stood, as it did 3,000 years before, but it was already in the last stages of decay, "its splendor of life had boiled over and wasted into steam and froth." Looking east, the Egyptian would see the ruins of other empires – the Hittites, the dreaded Assyrians were gone; mighty Babylon and mighty Egypt about to be absorbed into the Persian Empire.

As for the Greeks, like the ubiquitous Filipinos today, they were everywhere – in Egypt, Syria, Asia Minor, in hundreds of colonies scattered in the Aegean Islands and along the coasts from Marseilles to the Black Sea. They were an intelligent people, good mercenary soldiers, keen traders and skilled craftsmen. But there was also something irritating about their perpetual curiosity. Like the Filipinos, they always asking the reason for things, they poked around one's monuments, scrawled their names on the walls, pestered one with their eternal questions and chattered all the time.

How could one take them seriously? They were brave warriors and expert sailors, but far from falling in line behind a king like the obedient Egyptians and Babylonians, they could rarely be persuaded to even to follow their own clan leaders for long; they were perpetually quarrelling among themselves. The trouble was that they would argue and regard themselves as "free men" – whatever that meant.

"The Greeks are children, clever of course, but still children," said the Egyptian priest, as he would return to his temple to perform once again the sacred rites which his predecessors had been practicing since the dawn of history. *He* did not ask questions. His ancestors had provided all the answers more than 3,000 years ago.

"The Filipinos are children, how can we take them seriously?" asked the American as he watched us waxing hot and cold over Vietnam, Parity Rights and the Military Bases, constantly arguing and quarrelling among ourselves. And as he goes into his air-conditioned stone-proof ivory tower on Roxas Boulevard – he is totally unaware, as it may seem to the interplanetary philosopher in his UFO, totally unaware that perhaps the hand of Destiny might have touched the brow of his lowly little brown brother, as it did the ancient Greek, 2,500 years ago.

Time has no beginning, no end – only a perpetual unfolding. Nations are born, they grow old, and they will surely die – so it was with the empires of Egypt, Rome, Spain and America's own Mother Britain – so it will be with Russia, Red China and our own Mother America in the next Armageddon. But the Philippines is still undergoing its birth pains, and God willing, it will survive to greatness as did Ancient Greece. And why not? The torch of civilization has been passed in one unbroken line from the ancient civilizations of Egypt and Asia Minor to Greece, to Rome, to Spain and England, and to the USA – from mother to son, from colonizer to colonized – why not then to American's only ward, the Philippines, by happy coincidence also heir to Spain, in a future world no longer willing to accept the leadership of the white minority?

The British, the Dutch, the French colonizers only wanted to trade and to secure sources of raw materials, and left their colonies exactly the way they found them. Of all the colonial powers only Spain and the United States had the self-anointed mission to mold their colonies to their own image. The Philippines stands unique as the product of both Spanish and American colonizers. Spain gave us the Christianity and the United States our educational system and political democracy, the roots of which reach back to Ancient Greece, half a millennium before Christ.

So, my friends, let's swing our mind's eye about to a bygone era and take a look at the Ancient Greeks to seek if we can find in them some glimpse into the future of the Filipino people. Beyond Beethoven's transitional "panic and emptiness" lay, after all, the bold, affirmative and glorious finale of the Fifth Symphony.

The most perplexing contradiction in the character of the Ancient Greek, as it is with the Filipino, is between their capacity for rational thought, and their adherence to what we regard as the grossest superstition. They were probably the most intelligent and knowledgeable people that ever lived. They were founders of what we call "science"; they observed, studied and reasoned out things. They discovered the true nature of eclipses, that the world was round, and that, like the other planets, the earth revolved around the sun. They conducted deep inquiries about the origin of matter, calling the primal substance "*physis*" (nature, hence our word "physics"), made up of indivisible particles (from "*atomos*", meaning indivisible, comes our word "atom").

Yet these same brilliant people respected oracles, and could base vital decisions – such as whether or not to resist the Persians, and therefore whether or not Western Civilization should survive – on the babblings of an old woman squatting in a cave at Delphi, chewing laurel leaves.

There was never a unified Greek state. Partly because of the geography of the country, divided as it was, like the Philippines, by high mountains and sea channels running deep inland, and partly due to the character of the people themselves, the Greek ideal of government became the small, independent city state which they called *"polis"*; it is from this incidentally and related Greek words such as *"polites"* (citizen) and *"politeia"* (citizenship) that we derive our words "political" – pertaining to the state or its government – and "politician" – one allegedly skilled in politics. To the Greeks, the state was the city and its surrounding areas, most of them small, like our ancient Barangays.

Except for Sparta, the Greeks were not ruled by kings. They experimented with various forms of government, usually elective: sometimes an oligarchy (rule by a few), sometimes an aristocracy which originally meant "rule by the best" (from *"aristos"*, best and *"kratia"* rule), but often one man would seize power and became an absolute ruler (autocrat). The Greeks discovered –as who has not? – that such men are often corrupted by power, then the Greeks gave them the less complimentary name of *"turranikos"* (tyrant), meaning a cruel and oppressive ruler; and it became an act of patriotism to destroy them. The most popular form of government – in every sense of the word – was *"demokratia"* (rule by the people) which reached its greatest glory in Athens 450 years before Christ. From it comes our word "democracy". It is significant that all our words describing systems of government came from the Greek language. As with the Filipinos, the Greek ideal was the full complete man, daring, adventurous, sexy, successful in many fields of activity, in which wealth is acquired was merely incidental. ###

The ancient Greeks were, like the Filipino, a race of individualists. But this was a strength and a weakness, for while the Greek love of freedom gave full play to the growth of the spirit and of the intellect encouraging the gifted and the intelligent, it hindered them from uniting and sinking their differences in the face of a common enemy, except on one rare and wonderful occasion.

The finest in the Greek spirit showed itself in other ways. It took the dross of barbaric myth and the earth of folktale, and transmuted it into the pure gold of poetry. In the hands of Aeschylus, Euripides and Sophocles, poetic myth became an instrument which searched men's hearts and souls, making them see the splendor and the meanness, the tragedy and comedy of human life. The Oresteian trilogy of Aeschylus tells the story of cannibalism, human sacrifice, murder, matricide – as barbarous and inhuman as any folktale from Egypt.   Yet Aeschylus transforms into one of the greatest tragedies of the world, exploring the heights which the human spirit can attain, and the miry depths to which it can sink; its message, the futility of revenge, of violence breeding violence, war breeding war, is as pertinent today as it was 2,500 years ago.

"We love things of the mind," the Athenians (Ateneans to us) used to say, and sat at the feet of teachers and philosophers, Socrates, Plato and Aristotle. The ordinary Athenians, men and women, who crowded the open-air theater of Dionysus, on the slope of the Acropolis, did not mind being asked to think. Not that they went there for culture. They went there to be entertained, as we do when we go to movies or watch television (and by the way, Manila has more movie houses and television stations than most comparable cities in the world). In the theater of Dionysus – the birthplace of Western drama – they sat happily munching their figs and pomegranates, and was played out before them the tragedies of Aeschylus, Euripides' satires on public men (where politicians are subjected to barbs and lampoons, as in our modern Press Gridiron affairs). And they roared at the comedies of Aristophanes – sex comedies of such outrageous, glorious wit reminiscent of our own burlesques, starring Dolphy.

The classical Greeks were a different kind of human beings from any other that preceded them -- the Egyptians, the Sumerians, the Assyrians, the Babylonians – different in the art, their literature, moral outlook, political organization, in their way of thinking, and feeling about life. How did they get that way? First, they were great travelers and wherever they went they came in contact with earlier, older cultures which they approached with fresh curious minds untrammeled by traditions. Secondly, there was the so-called "genius of the race". Theories of racial superiority tend to be discredited nowadays, but I do believe that the Greeks, especially of Athens, possessed special qualities of mind and character which enabled them to make full use of their opportunities. Since men first achieved civilization there has never been such a flowering of genius as occurred, within one century, in Athens of 450 BC. In a city no larger than Pasay City – only three generations produced such tragic poets as

Aeschylus, Euripides and Sophocles, and the comic poet Aristophanes; philosophers such as Socrates, Plato, Aristotle, Anaxagoras; the great Herodotus, the father of historians; the sculptors Phidias and Praxiteles; and statesmen of the quality of Pericles and Themistocles. These were only the most distinguished. There are many others who, in a less brilliant age, would have shone as brightly as Christopher Marlowe and Ben Johnson might have done, had they not lived in the Age of William Shakespeare. ###

A historian once remarked: "It is as though the individuality of the Greek civilization strove for a brief period of its maturity to surpass the bounds of possible achievement."

Could this be said of us Filipinos too – that in a brief period of half a century, we surpassed the bounds of possible achievement – producing Jose Rizal, Claro M. Recto, Andres Bonifacio, Emilio Aguinaldo, Manuel L. Quezon, Juan Luna, Jose Diokno, Ninoy Aquino, Nick Joaquin, Frank Sionil Jose – all in three generations? That in a brief period of our maturity, we were the first Asian nation to break the shackles of Western Colonialism and declare our independence, establish a constitutional democracy, antedating Sun Yat Sen and the Chinese Double Tenth by 13 years? That almost a century later, we followed it up with the Edsa Revolution, the very first in history to depose a dictator by peaceful means, followed moment by moment by an astonished world audience through a new international Television Network, and followed as an example by a wave of peaceful revolutions that destroyed the Communist world?

Or is our greatest glory yet to come? And our tragedy yet to follow?

The victory of the Greeks at Marathon and Salamis over the Persian brand of colonial Imperialism did not bring the millennium to Greece. Greek individualism and self-interest, the stubborn pride that had beaten the barbarian, broke up in the end the precious unity Athens had striven to create. Greek fought Greek, for power, for possession of land, out of jealousy of Athen's dominance. Men fought and died bravely, but year after year the Hellenic world dissipated its strength in war. And weakened, it was finally destroyed. But that is another story. ***

The ancient Greeks are a people whom we Filipinos recognize, and who, despite many differences, think, act and speak like us. One not only admires, but loves them – and despairs for them. They had all our faults; perhaps we have a few of their virtues – one hopes so.

We Filipinos who travel to Greece, as Herodotus once travelled to the ancient civilizations of Egypt and Babylon, we may find in Greece the very roots of our being. We find here the remains of temples and monuments, still standing, gloriously arrayed by the majesty of time. It seems that the flower of youth throbs within them, which time cannot quell, as if there flowed through their stone the immortal breath of a soul rebellious to age.

And as we gaze at the Acropolis high on the crest of a towering rock of ages, we hear the echo of words spoken down the corridors of time. And if we Filipinos listen carefully, they seem to be saying to us especially:

I am the Glory that was Greece. For centuries past and for eons to come, I shall stand for order, law and clarity. I shall be a manner of thought, of love, of reason.

Lifting their eyes towards me, philosophers shall discover the depths of thought, architects shall dream of the majesty of their palaces.

So come to me, all you truth-seekers.

Come to this consecrated rock – where truth, virtue and infinite beauty have mingled to give birth to the Consciousness of Man.

January 4-8, 2016

Part 2. The Balfour Declaration of 1917, Why Hitler hated the Jews

It was a very short letter, about half a page, dated 2 November 1917, signed by the United Kingdom's Foreign Secretary Arthur James Balfour, and sent to the Jewish Zionist Federation through Baron Rothschild, leader of the British Jewish community, promising a "homeland" for the Jews in Palestine. Known as the Balfour Declaration, it set into motion the most wicked and cruel genocide in history known as the Holocaust, and then placed the Jewish people at the center of a Muslim holy war (jihad) that threatens the peace of the entire world.

At the time, while the Jews faced a lot of anti-Semitic prejudice all over Christendom, they were comparatively better treated in Germany and Austria. Jews experienced a period of ostensible legal equality from 1848 until the rise of Nazi Germany. In the opinion of historian Fritz Stern, by the end of the 19th century, what had emerged was a Jewish-German symbiosis, where German Jews had merged elements of German and Jewish culture into a unique new one. Marriages between Jews and non-Jews became somewhat common from the 19th century; for example, the wife of German Chancellor Gustav Stresemann was Jewish. More German Jews, like Albert Einstein and Karl Marx. were involved in scientific and sociological research than in any other country. A higher percentage of German Jews fought in World War I than that of any other ethnic, religious or political group in Germany; some 12,000 died for their country. Ironically, it was a Jewish lieutenant, Hugo Gutmann, who awarded the Iron Cross, First Class, to a 29-year-old corporal named Adolf Hitler.

The Balfour Declaration was intended to ensure the loyalty of the International Jews to the cause of Great Britain during World War I, not only in the United States where Jews predominate in the film industry, in banking and judicial circles, but also in Germany. When Germany lost the war, the German Jews were accused of lack of patriotism, and "stab in the back" allegations. The Allies were harsh in treating their erstwhile enemies, and plagued with economic hardships, the Germans accused the Jews of getting rich on the plight of the Germans. Thus was born the Nazi Movement that climaxed with the Final Solution in mass concentration camps.

The British were not serious about the Balfour Declaration. Only a generation later after World War II, did the United Nations under pressure from the Jewish lobby in the United States, granted international Jews a nation by dismembering Palestine. The long suffering Arabs long exploited by the West for their oil, had to face an Israel armed by the United States with nuclear weapons. Thus the Muslim Jihad came into being. Israel, with the help of the powerful Jewish lobby in the USA is now the tail that wags the American dog.

December 21, 2012

3.   From barbarism to decadence without being civilized

After raving about Filipino men who do nothing all day but pet their cocks (huh?) while their women do all the work, Will

numerous awards and testimonials.
February 10, 1987

ooooo

END OF BOOK